Don & Louise
Wells

CU00921494

LIVES OF GREAT RELIGIOUS BOOKS

The *Book of Common Prayer*

LIVES OF GREAT RELIGIOUS BOOKS

The *Book of Common Prayer*

A BIOGRAPHY

Alan Jacobs

PRINCETON UNIVERSITY PRESS

Princeton and Oxford

Published by Princeton University Press, 41 William Street,
Princeton, New Jersey 08540
In the United Kingdom: Princeton University Press,
6 Oxford Street, Woodstock, Oxfordshire OX20 1TW
press.princeton.edu

Jacket photograph: *Book of Common Prayer*, 1662. Courtesy of the Underwood
Prayer Book Collection of the Francis Donaldson Library at Nashotah House
Theological Seminary. Photography by Bliss Lemmon.

Library of Congress Cataloging-in-Publication Data

Jacobs, Alan, 1958–
    The Book of Common Prayer : a biography / Alan Jacobs.
        pages   cm. — (Lives of great religious books)
    Includes index.
    Summary: "While many of us are familiar with such famous words as, "Dear-
ly beloved, we are gathered together here." or "Ashes to ashes, dust to dust," we
may not know that they originated with The Book of Common Prayer, which
first appeared in 1549. Like the words of the King James Bible and Shakespeare,
the language of this prayer book has saturated English culture and letters. Here
Alan Jacobs tells its story. Jacobs shows how The Book of Common Prayer—
from its beginnings as a means of social and political control in the England of
Henry VIII to its worldwide presence today—became a venerable work whose
cadences express the heart of religious life for many. The book's chief maker,
Thomas Cranmer, Archbishop of Canterbury, created it as the authoritative
manual of Christian worship throughout England. But as Jacobs recounts,
the book has had a variable and dramatic career in the complicated history of
English church politics, and has been the focus of celebrations, protests, and
even jail terms. As time passed, new forms of the book were made to suit the
many English-speaking nations: first in Scotland, then in the new United States,
and eventually wherever the British Empire extended its arm. Over time, Cranmer's book was adapted for different preferences and purposes. Jacobs vividly
demonstrates how one book became many—and how it has shaped the devotional lives of men and women across the globe"—Provided by publisher.
    ISBN 978-0-691-15481-7 (hardback)
    1. Anglican Communion—Liturgy—Texts—History.   2. Church of Eng-
land. Book of common prayer—History.   I. Title.
    BX5145.J27 2013
    264'.03009—dc23

                                                        2013019886

British Library Cataloging-in-Publication Data is available

This book has been composed in Garamond Premier Pro
Printed on acid-free paper. ∞
Printed in the United States of America
10 9 8 7 6 5 4 3 2

for Wesley

CONTENTS

1544 Thomas Cranmer composes and promulgates the Great Litany

1549 the first *Book of Common Prayer* published

1552 second *Book of Common Prayer* published

1553 proscription of the *Book of Common Prayer* by Queen Mary

1559 the Elizabethan *Book of Common Prayer* published

1604 Hampton Court Conference convened by King James I

1637 a Scottish *Book of Common Prayer* promulgated and rescinded

1641 the *Book of Common Prayer* proscribed by Parliament

1662 the post-Restoration revision of the *Book of Common Prayer* completed and promulgated

1789 the first American *Book of Common Prayer* published

1928 a revised *Book of Common Prayer* published
      in America; a revised book fails to pass Parliament in Britain
1945 Gregory Dix publishes *The Shape of the Liturgy*
1954 first liturgies of the Church of South India's
      Book of Common Worship published
1964 *A Liturgy for Africa* published
1979 revised American *Book of Common Prayer*
      published
1980 the Church of England publishes the *Alternative Service Book*
2000 the *Common Worship* project replaces the ASB;
      its work is now ongoing

LIST OF FIGURES

In quoting from the early versions of the *Book of Common Prayer*, from 1549 to 1662, I use the superb recent edition edited by Brian Cummings, *The Book of Common Prayer: The Texts of 1549, 1559, and 1662* (Oxford: Oxford University Press, 2011). In citing it I use the abbreviation BCP followed by the page number. While Cummings preserves the original spelling, I have generally modernized it slightly in the cause of readability.

Two other books have been constantly open on my desk during the writing of this book, and I have cited them frequently enough that they deserve their own abbreviations as well. One is Diarmaid MacCulloch's *Thomas Cranmer: A Life* (New Haven, CT: Yale University Press, 1996), which shall be known here as TC. The other is *The Oxford Guide to the Book of Common Prayer: A Worldwide Survey*, edited by Charles Helfling and Cynthia Shattuck (New York: Oxford University Press, 2006), which I mark as OG, though adding the author and full title of each essay I quote.

The *Book of Common Prayer*

The Archbishop in His Library

The archbishop's palace at Croydon, south of London, sat amid low-lying woods. King Henry avoided it: of another palace belonging to the archbishop he commented, "This house standeth low and is rheumatic, like unto Croydon, where I could never be without sickness."[1] But it was here that Thomas Cranmer, Archbishop of Canterbury, kept a great library; it was here that he sifted through his vast treasure-store of biblical commentary, theology, and manuals of worship. Many of his books were very old and reflected the forms of Catholic liturgy and teaching that had dominated Europe for centuries; these had generally been written by the patient hands of monastic scribes. Others had come quite recently from the printing press and embodied the great debates that absorbed Christians throughout Europe. There were texts by Martin Luther and his followers, and by the great humanist Erasmus of Rotterdam (whom Cranmer had long admired), and by leading Catholic thinkers like the reforming Spaniard Cardinal Quiñones. Books of worship made in centuries past by Cranmer's fellow Englishmen—missals and breviaries, psalters and processionals, composed in all corners of the kingdom, from Bangor to York—were well represented. There were Bibles too, some of them in English; in 1540 Cranmer had written a preface to the one known as the Great Bible.[2]

The year was, let us say, 1543. Cranmer had made his first bold drafts of an English liturgy in 1538, but that work was not well received by the few who saw it, and he had learned to be more cautious. He sat at his desk and studied his books and thought of how he might produce a liturgy in English that would please a king whose moods and inclinations had become ever harder to predict. Henry had injured his leg at a tournament in 1536, and the wound had never healed; he had become fatter and fatter, probably gouty as well, and could scarcely move. For some years his attitudes toward reforming the church had vacillated. In the aftermath of the Act of Supremacy in 1534, which made him the head of the English Church and denied to the Church at Rome any authority in England, he showed some Reforming sympathies, but as time had gone by his love of older ways, and the old church language of Latin, had returned. After all, Christian worship in England had been conducted in Latin for a thousand years or more. Cranmer therefore understood the challenge of composing an English liturgy capable of gaining Henry's wholehearted approval.

We cannot guess with any degree of confidence how Cranmer calculated. He is one of the more inscrutable characters in English history, whose actions at times seem guileful, disingenuous, or temporizing and at other times doggedly persistent and deeply principled. All we know is that in the end he chose to compose a Litany, and that few other choices would have been so agreeable to the king.

A Litany consists of a series of petitions to God: they are spoken by a priest and affirmed by the people in a fixed refrain. The mood is generally sober, penitential; the Litany was traditionally said or sung in procession, and in 1544, when this one was first published and used, these processions would have been enacted throughout much of England. Henry, still determined to reject papal leadership, and contemplating war with France, was surely delighted to hear the priest call out,

> That it may please thee to keep Henry the viii.
>   thy servant and our king and governor:
> That it may please thee to rule his heart in thy
>   faith, fear, and love that he may ever have affi-
>   ance in [that is, reliance on] thee, & ever seek
>   thy honor & glory:
> That it may please thee to be his defender and
>   keeper, giving him the victory over all his
>   enemies:

and after each plea to hear the people cry,

> *We beseech thee to hear us good Lord.*[3]

Earlier in the litany the people had prayed for deliverance "from blindness of heart, from pride, vainglory, and hypocrisy, from envy, hatred and malice, and all uncharitableness," but also "from all sedition and privy conspiracy, [and] from the tyranny of the bishop of Rome and all his detestable enormities." This was a service well designed indeed to win Henry's sympathy.

As Thomas Cranmer sat at his desk at Croydon Palace, he wove this rite from many sources: little in it was uniquely his own, and its deepest roots are ancient. After the opening invocation of God as Trinity comes the first great plea: "Remember not Lord our offenses, nor the offenses of our forefathers, neither take thou vengeance of our sins," which echoes the ancient prayers of Israel. "O remember not the sins & offenses of my youth, but according unto thy mercy think upon me (O Lord) for thy goodness" says Psalm 25, as rendered in the Great Bible. Or Psalm 79: "O remember not our old sins, but have mercy upon us, and that soon, for we are come to great misery." The very first line of the Litany, "O god, the father of heaven, have mercy upon us miserable sinners," derives from Jesus's story of the Pharisee and the tax collector (Luke 18). And much of the rest of the Litany is a straight translation from a rite created at Sarum, near modern Salisbury, in the eleventh or twelfth century. Cranmer was not even original in putting these various pieces together: something similar had been done by William Marshall, an Englishman of Lutheran inclinations, in his *Godly Primer* of 1535.[4]

Yet for all its modesty and derivativeness, Cranmer's 1544 Litany was the beginning of something very big indeed. That single rite would be the first installment of a book, the *Book of Common Prayer*, that would transform the religious lives of countless English men, women, and children; that would mark the lives of millions as they moved through the stages of life from birth and baptism through marriage and on to illness and death and burial; that would accompany the British Empire as it expanded throughout the world. When Cranmer was still alive a version of that book was the first book printed in Ireland; a quarter-century after his death prayers from it were read in what we now call California by the chaplain of Sir Francis Drake; and versions of it are used today in Christian churches all over the world, as far from England as South Africa, Singapore, and New Zealand. That book's rite of marriage has become for many people, Christian and non-Christian alike, *the* means by which two people are joined: I participated many years ago in a Unitarian wedding in Tulsa, Oklahoma, that began with the minister's intoning of the familiar words: "Dearly beloved, we are gathered together here in the sight of God, and in the face of this congregation, to join together this man and this woman in holy Matrimony."

Whatever Cranmer was thinking when he sat among his books in Croydon Palace, in "an obscure and darke place" surrounded by trees, whatever he thought might come of his little exercise in vernacular rite-making, he was imagining nothing even remotely like what would come to pass.

FIGURE 1. Portrait of Thomas Cranmer, Archbishop of
Canterbury, by Gerlach Flicke, painted near the end of the
reign of Henry VIII. Cranmer is holding the letters of St. Paul,
and one of the books on the table before him is St. Augustine's
De Fide Et Operibus ("On Faith and Works").

© National Portrait Gallery, London

One Book for One Country

The *Book of Common Prayer* came into being as an instrument of social and political control. There will be much else to say about its origins, but here we must begin: the prayer book was a key means by which the great lords who ruled on behalf of the young King Edward VI consolidated English rule of the English church. In making one book according to which the whole country would worship, Cranmer and his allies were quite consciously dismantling an immense and intricate edifice of devotional practice. They had both theological and political reasons for doing this, but the immediate effect was political and was widely seen as such.

Only the barest outlines of this ever-branching network of conflicts can be traced here. The story effectively begins with Henry VIII, though Henry was not the first to insist on English rule of the English church: throughout the fourteenth century Parliament had passed laws limiting the scope of papal power in England, culminating in the great

Statute of *Praemunire*, enacted as law at the very end of that century, during the reign of Richard II. Such laws had been prompted by royal resentment of the pope's power to appoint non-Englishmen to highly profitable ecclesiastical offices, but Henry VIII drew on these precedents to argue that the pope had no right to determine whether Henry was legally married to Catherine of Aragon, whom he had wed in 1509. After a series of miscarriages and infant deaths—Prince Henry, the longed-for heir to the throne, died in 1511 after just a few days of life—King Henry came to believe that his marriage to Catherine was unlawful and displeasing to God. Catherine had been married to Henry's older brother, Arthur, and according to the notions of consanguinity then followed she and Henry could not marry after Arthur's death. This prohibition had been lifted by Pope Julius II, but by 1527 Henry was openly arguing not only that Julius had been wrong to permit the marriage—in direct violation of Leviticus 20:21, as Henry interpreted the text—but also, and more important, that Julius had never possessed legitimate authority in the matter. The legal tradition embodied in the *praemunire* laws made it clear, Henry said, that no pope could make such determinations about the marriage of an English king. So he wanted his marriage annulled, and moreover demanded that the current pope, Clement VII, agree that Julius had exceeded his authority in proclaiming lawful Henry's marriage to Catherine.

Of course, Henry also wished to marry Anne Boleyn.

Assisted by his leading minister, Cardinal Wolsey—and later, after Wolsey's fall from grace due to his failure to resolve the king's "Great Matter," by Thomas Cromwell—Henry sought to convince English churchmen that the king was "the only protector and supreme head of the English church and clergy," and that the church itself could only hold such powers "which do not disparage the regal authority and laws."[1] The churchmen resisted, to varying degrees, as did Parliament when its prerogatives were involved, though Henry's warning to them in 1532 had been blunt: "I assure you, if you will not take some reasonable end now when it is offered, I will search out the extremity of the law, and then will I not offer you so much again." And indeed, eventually Henry got what he wanted. They key year for resolving the Great Matter, and for many future matters also, was 1533. On March 30, Thomas Cranmer—strongly supported by the Boleyn family—was installed as Archbishop of Canterbury, swearing an oath that he would not allow his loyalty to the church to trump his loyalty to the king, and pledging that he would do nothing to interfere with "reformation of the Christian religion, the government of the English Church, or the prerogative of the Crown or the well-being of the same commonwealth." Soon thereafter Parliament passed a law allowing ecclesiastical suits to be tried in England, by English clergy, and on May 23, Cranmer, having heard the evidence in the case, declared King Henry's marriage to Catherine null and void. This would have paved the way for Henry to marry Anne, except that, anticipating all these events, Henry had already done so in January. In September Anne gave birth to Elizabeth, the future Virgin Queen.

All the pieces were in place for the emergence of an English Reformation, the establishment of the Church of England, and the creation of the *Book of Common Prayer*, but none of these events was clearly foreseen by anyone. Some of the thinkers Henry had relied on to consolidate his case were closely associated with the nascent Protestant Reformation: as early as 1528 Anne Boleyn had lent Henry a copy of *The Obedience of a Christian Man* by William Tyndale, a radical theologian in exile on the Continent and the first great translator of the Bible into modern English. Of Tyndale's *Obedience* Henry is alleged to have said, "This is a book for me, and for all kings to read," but about the Reformation project as a whole he wavered, doubtful.

Henry practiced theology long before he anointed himself head of the English Church; in 1521 he had written *Assertio septem sacramentorum* (Defense of the Seven Sacraments), a refutation of Martin Luther that led Rome to proclaim him "Defender of the Faith," and some of his later theological interventions also revealed a traditionalist bent. But not all. As his reign progressed Henry's theological proclamations became more forceful and more incoherent. He passionately defended transubstantiation—the conversion during the Mass of bread and wine into the body and blood of Christ—but with equal passion denounced the worship of images and denied the power of relics. He thought of the priesthood more as an administrative position than a divine vocation, yet demanded that priests remain celibate, on penalty of death. (When this insistence became law in 1539, as part of the so-called Six Articles, Thomas Cranmer felt the need to smuggle his wife and children out of the country.) Henry may have venerated Tyndale's *Obedience of a Christian Man*, but in 1536 he at least acquiesced in Tyndale's execution, despite Thomas Cromwell's pleas on the reformer's behalf. Henry consistently despised what he believed to be the pernicious doctrine of justification by faith alone, a point on which, perhaps surprisingly, Cranmer ventured to argue with the king. The Ten Articles, published by Cranmer in 1536 at the king's insistence, defended the cult of the saints, but two years later, as part of the dissolution and despoliation of the English monasteries, Henry destroyed the shrine of St. Thomas à Becket at Canterbury, disinterred and destroyed the saint's bones, and forbade the very mention of the man's name. (Thomas, as an exemplar of pious resistance to an overreaching king, and as the most famous of all English saints, represented a greater threat to Henry's program than any other holy figure.) By 1545, in the *King's Primer*, whose authorship Henry claimed, prayers for the dead were mocked: "There is nothing in the Dirge taken out of Scripture that maketh any mention of the souls departed than doth the tale of Robin Hood." One may discern in these assertions—wildly varying in their theological tendencies but unanimous in their dictatorial tone—a slow drift toward the Reformers, but that is the most that can be said.

However, throughout the last fifteen years of Henry's reign the evangelical party gradually consolidated its hold on the English church and on some of the nation's leading aristocratic families.[2] When Henry died in 1547, leaving his throne to nine-year-old Edward, the son his third wife, Jane Seymour, had borne him, the evangelicals found themselves with free rein to reshape the English church. They took full advantage of the opportunity.

📖

For our purposes here, the key role played by the council of regents, who ruled England on behalf of young King Edward, was to leave Thomas Cranmer the freedom to make such changes to the doctrine, worship, and structure of English Christianity as he saw fit to make. And he saw fit to make many. Henry may have insisted on the reassertion of many traditionalist positions in the Ten Articles of 1536 and the Six Articles of 1539, but throughout the latter part of Henry's reign Cranmer was at work, quietly and slowly, implementing countervailing changes.[3]

It was actually Thomas Cromwell in 1538 who authorized, on behalf of the king, the printing, distribution, and use of an English Bible—what would come to be called the Great Bible—as translated by Miles Coverdale. Coverdale, working on the Continent as Tyndale had and drawing heavily on Tyndale's work, had published a complete English Bible in 1535 and several updated versions since. (Coverdale knew little Hebrew or Greek, and relied on the Latin Vulgate and on Luther's German Bible to finish Tyndale's work.) He oversaw the printing of the Great Bible in Paris and had the copies shipped across the Channel. By the king's order, a copy of the Great Bible was displayed in every parish church in England, chained to a desk so it might be read by any and all—or, since most parishioners were illiterate, so it could be seen. Priests were required to read the biblical passages appointed for any given service in Coverdale's English.

So by the time Cranmer's English version of the Litany came to be used in 1544, English Christians were getting used to English accompanying Latin in their worship services. There was no overnight replacement of Latin by English, but rather a gradual process by which Latin receded and English became more dominant. That was how Cranmer preferred to get things done. He worked on English versions of a revised breviary (a book containing the Daily Office, the prayers priests say at various times each day) and a primer (a book adapted from the breviary for the use of laypersons in their private prayers). When these did not gain immediate acceptance, he set them aside and turned to other tasks. Concerning the most explosive matters he simply remained silent: though scholars now believe that by Henry's death he had come to disbelieve that Christ was corporeally present in any way in the Mass, he knew that Henry's commitment to the doctrine was so absolute that debate was futile at best and mortally dangerous at worst. He bided his time.

He served the king obediently even in matters that must have wounded his conscience. Although he protested the execution of Thomas Cromwell, he dared not deny the charges made against Henry's longtime chief minister. In 1542 he interrogated Henry's fifth queen, Katherine Howard, and secured her confession to the capital crime of adultery; this could not have given him any real satisfaction, much less pleasure. But by obedience, and by keeping a remarkably low profile when traditionalists hunted (sometimes successfully) for heretics among his fellow evangelicals, he kept the cause of reform alive and always moving, however imperceptibly, forward. In 1545 Cranmer commissioned a portrait of himself by a German artist, Gerlach Flicke. It shows him sitting, holding open a book of the epistles of St. Paul. On the table before him lies a book by St. Augustine, *De fide et operibus*—On Faith and Works. Paul and Augustine were of course the prime authorities on whose thought the Reformation was built, and more specifically were the chief articulators of the gospel of justification *sola fide*, by faith alone. On this point Cranmer staked not only his reputation but also his whole public identity. He could wait as long as necessary to bring this point home to the English people. He bided his time and when Edward came to the throne he could at last act swiftly and decisively.

On January 28, 1547, as Henry lay dying, Cranmer sat with him and held his hand. The archbishop did not conduct any of the familiar Catholic prayers for the dying, but asked the king to make some sign that he placed his trust in Jesus Christ. Henry squeezed Cranmer's hand, and then died.[4] At the coronation of Henry's young son, Edward, Cranmer delivered a homily encouraging the new king to be like Josiah, King of Judah, who also came to the throne as a boy but then went on to lead a revival of true religion in his country (as described in 2 Kings 22). Having so exhorted his new sovereign, Cranmer set to work.

One can understand a good deal of what Cranmer would seek to achieve in making a prayer book by noting one of his first major actions under Edward: overseeing the creation of a *Book of Homilies*. For Cranmer, traditional religion in England had been more concerned to demonstrate the sacerdotal power of the priesthood than to instruct the people in Christian doctrine and practice. Sermons were rarely preached, and when preached were rarely doctrinally sound or useful. The *Book of Homilies* was meant to remedy that deficiency. Moreover, one can see Cranmer's chief concerns by the order of the Homilies, especially the first four, which he almost certainly composed:

A Fruitful exhortation to the reading of holy
  Scripture.
Of the misery of all mankind.
Of the salvation of all mankind.
Of the true and lively faith.
Of good works.
Of Christian love and charity.
Against swearing and perjury.
Of the declining from GOD.
An exhortation against the fear of death.
An exhortation to obedience.
Against whoredom and adultery.
Against strife and contention.

It is the reading of the Bible that Cranmer first wants to ensure. (He had already emphasized the same point in his 1540 preface to the Great Bible.) The principles of evangelical theology are laid out in neat sequence here: Read the Bible and you will learn of "the misery of all mankind," that all since Adam's fall suffer under the power of sin; you will also learn that God has made one plan for "the salvation of all mankind" in the death and resurrection of his son Jesus Christ; and you will further learn that the only way to grasp this salvation is by having a "true and lively faith" in Christ as your Savior. Moreover, "good works" do not lead to this faith, they follow from it: a genuine faith will "break out and shew itself by good works," but salvation is by God's grace alone (*sola gratia*) and again, this grace is appropriated by the believer through faith alone (*sola fide*). It was necessary, thought Cranmer, that this plan of salvation be universally understood, and the first requirement of that understanding was the reading of Scripture. The commissioning, writing, and promulgating of these homilies occupied much of Cranmer's time in 1547.

Meanwhile, he pursued a more obviously momentous task that he must have been contemplating—and probably had been privately working on—for some years: "The Order of the Communion," that is, an English liturgy for the part of the traditional Mass during which laypersons receive the bread and wine. Or rather, the bread: it had for centuries been customary for laypersons to receive Communion rarely, perhaps once a year, and in "one kind," but Cranmer was determined to make Communion much more frequent, to have it administered "in both kinds," and to create an English liturgy that would explain to laypersons what precisely they were and were not doing when they consumed the elements. On Easter Sunday 1548, by order of the Archbishop of Canterbury, this English order for Communion became mandatory throughout England. The Latin Mass that had, in its various forms, been the only Mass in England for nearly a millennium was at that one stroke abolished.

Over the past quarter-century a great deal of scholarly work has been done on the devotional world of late medieval England, most notably by Eamon Duffy in his brilliant, polemical, and influential study *The Stripping of the Altars*. Duffy and a number of other scholars have given us a vivid picture of ordinary late medieval English folk at prayer, and it is only by taking at least a brief glance at that picture that we will be able to understand just how dramatically Cranmer and the other evangelical leaders of England changed the country's religious experience.

It was long commonplace to think of the Middle Ages as a period of collective, communal experience, and the rise of modernity in the sixteenth century as heralding a new era of individualism. But in terms of public prayer, something like the opposite was true. The High Mass in particular was generally understood as an opportunity for private devotion. It was true that the priest celebrated the Mass in a language the common people did not understand, but in practice his performance of the rite on behalf of the congregants left them free to engage, if they wished, in deep silent or whispered prayer. The priest's gestures and intonations were sufficient for people to understand the major transitions in the rite and adjust their devotions accordingly. But throughout most of the Mass, the people were allowed and encouraged to lose themselves in prayer, often with assistance from their rosary beads. Cranmer's great nemesis, the traditionalist bishop Stephen Gardiner, called special attention to these habits: "In times past, when men came to church more diligently than some do now, the people in the church took small heed what the priest and the clerks did in the chancel, but only to stand up at the Gospel and kneel at the Sacring," that is, the moment of transubstantiation of bread into Christ's flesh.

For Gardiner and other traditionalist bishops, it seemed evident that celebrating the Eucharistic rite in English would only distract people from their prayers. John Christopherson, the dean of Norwich, wrote in 1554 that the congregation should "travail themselves in fervent praying, and so shall they highly please God. . . . It is much better for them not to understand the common service of the church, because when they hear others praying in a loud voice, in the language that they understand, they are [hindered] from prayer themselves, and so come they to such a slackness and negligence in praying, that at length as we have well seen in these late days, in manner pray not at all." So also the Catholic controversialist Thomas Harding: "as the vulgar service"— that is, the service in English—"pulleth their minds from private devotion to hear and not to pray, to little benefit of knowledge, for the obscurity of it; so the Latin giveth them no such motion."[5]

For Cranmer and his fellow evangelicals, these traditional practices turned what should have been an experience of communal devotion, a shared experience of gratitude for God's mercies, into a kind of magic show. In 1543, when Cranmer had experimented with an English liturgy in parishes in Kent, the people were deeply dubious that the Lord's Prayer said in English would *work*: their feeling was that the incantation had to be said precisely, and in Latin.[6] Likewise, many historians have surmised that the phrase "hocus pocus" is a corruption of *Hoc est corpus meum*, "This is my body": Christ's words instituting the practice of Communion, and the words uttered by the priest at the Sacring. The common practice at High Mass was for the priest to "elevate" the Host at this moment, so that people might "see their Lord"—especially important since they were unlikely to be receiving the bread. (As Eamon Duffy has pointed out, in a low Mass, conducted daily and perhaps in a side chapel of the parish church, the experience was much more intimate: people crowded close to the altar, drawing as near as possible to the consecrated elements, which they nevertheless did not touch or taste.[7]) Cranmer found all this deeply exasperating and alien to genuine Christian devotion. In his book *Defence of the True and Catholic Doctrine of the Sacrament of the Body and Blood of Christ* (1550, though written in 1548), he writes,

> What made the people to run from their seats to the altar, and from altar to altar, and from sacring (as they called it) to sacring, peeping, tooting and gazing at that thing which the priest held up

in his hands, if they thought not to honour the thing which they saw? What moved the priests to lift up the sacrament so high over their heads? Or the people to say to the priest, "Hold up! Hold up!"; or one man to say to another "Stoop down before"; or to say "This day have I seen my Maker"; and "I cannot be quiet except I see my Maker once a day"? What was the cause of all these, and that as well the priest and the people so devoutly did knock and kneel at every sight of the sacrament, but that they worshipped that visible thing which they saw with their eyes and took it for very God?[8]

For Cranmer there was no transubstantiation, hence no Lord to be seen in the bread; instead, the traditional Mass offered at best a series of distractions from the real business of understanding and giving thanks for the grace offered to the faithful believer in Christ; at worst—and he was inclined to believe the worst—it was the sheerest idolatry.

Of course, the parishioners themselves rarely entered such debates; they just knew that a structure of devotional experience they had known all their lives, as their ancestors had before them, was being pulled down around their heads. It is impossible to guess how many of them regretted this demolition. The standard view for many years—as exemplified in A. G. Dickens's venerable *The English Reformation* (1964)—was that while some traditionalists complained, and the ecclesiastical powers wished to preserve their reputations as powerful magicians, the majority of English Christians welcomed the English liturgies as a deliverance from priestly domination and as an opportunity for deeper devotion. By contrast, Duffy argues in *The Stripping of the Altars* that only a few radicals welcomed the changes, while the majority grieved at being deprived of their familiar spiritual comforts.[9]

Given that the great majority of human beings throughout history have been highly vulnerable to unexpected changes in weather, and to illness brought into the local community by strangers, and to the thousand other natural shocks that flesh is heir to, and have therefore been temperamentally inclined to conservatism, Duffy's view is intuitively more plausible. But whether natural conservatism applies in this particular case depends on the extent to which Reformation ideas had spread throughout the populace, so that ordinary people could come to envision the benefits of a change in traditional practice. And that, it turns out, is extremely hard to discern on a nationwide basis, though the preferences of some particular communities are known. We cannot therefore say with any confidence whether the changes Cranmer imposed were generally welcome or generally unwelcome. We can, though, say with near-absolute confidence that Cranmer did not care. He was not, it seems, a cruel or thoughtless man, and would probably have wanted to mitigate any pain and confusion resulting from the imposition of a new system of worship, but there is no indication that he ever doubted that such imposition was necessary.

Neither did the regents who ruled the nation doubt. From a late modern perspective, shaped by the separation of church and state, it might seem that the politicians' reasons for imposing a new model differed from that of the churchmen. In this account, the politicians required a uniform practice of belief as a means of forging a common English cultural identity that would stifle and then eliminate rival allegiances, especially to the church of Rome; churchmen like Cranmer, by contrast, wanted Christian truth to be unfailingly proclaimed and error suppressed so that people might know God and inherit eternal life. But for Cranmer as Archbishop of Canterbury under the developing Tudor system, these considerations joined hands. Centuries earlier, when Thomas à Becket had been archbishop and Henry II king, it had been impossible that the rights and privileges of the church *not* come into conflict with the rights and privileges of the state, and those conflicts had become no less complex as the modern state began gradually to emerge in the early modern period. Henry VIII had chosen to deal with this by declaring himself the head of the English church, which made that church local, not universal, and effectively a department of the state. Within this system it was completely logical that decisions should be made not for Christ's Church as a whole but only for its local, English, instantiation, *and* that within the realm those decisions should have uniform and absolute force.

So for Cranmer the Latinate heterogeneity of English worship was not politically *or* theologically problematic, or even politically *and* theologically problematic; rather, he would say, it was necessary *for the English church*, a theologico-political entity, that worship be embodied by one book, in one language, that mandated one use.

📖

A "use" in this context is a fixed way of doing liturgical business. Since the early days of the church, there had been very general agreement about what Christian worship ought to look like. The Eucharistic service had two big parts: first, the reading and preaching of the Word of God, coupled with communal prayers; the second, the sacramental liturgy proper. (In the very early church it was common for anyone to participate in the first part, but the unbaptized were shooed out and the door locked before the Holy Mysteries were enacted.) Certain liturgical moments became nearly universal: the "peace," for instance, where the congregants "greet one another with a holy kiss," according to St. Paul's commandment in Romans 16:16; the reciting of the Lord's Prayer; the reading out of Christ's words of institution, as recorded in each of the Synoptic Gospels and repeated by Paul in 1 Corinthians 11. But these were not performed in the same order everywhere and were accompanied by a variety of other elements. Similarly, as monastic culture developed, the "canonical hours" of daily prayer arose: a relatively but not absolutely standard sequence and a variety of ways to pray through that sequence. Episcopal governance brought, at most, uniformity within particular areas. Different parts of the world followed different uses, both in Eucharistic worship and in the daily office.

Thus when Cranmer rose to his archepiscopal seat, he might have heard Latin employed everywhere in England, but otherwise a wide range of practice. As he later wrote, when his liturgical revisions were mostly complete and the *Book of Common Prayer* ready for distribution, "Heretofore, there hath been great diversity in saying and singing in churches within this realm: some following Salisbury use, some Hereford use, same the use of Bangor, some of York, and some of Lincoln." (In Scotland the Sarum rite was the norm, in part because the Scots refused to be dictated to by York; but as Scotland was then its own kingdom, Cranmer need not concern himself with it.) So the Easter 1548 promulgation of his "Order of the Communion" was not just concerned to shift worship services from Latin to English; it was the first unambiguous indication that Cranmer meant *all* the public services everywhere in England to be conducted identically. "Now from henceforth, all the whole realm shall have but one use."[10]

Perhaps even more important to Cranmer than the establishment of one use was the regularization of the Kalendar, including what we now call the lectionary: the set of prescribed readings from Scripture. We have already seen that the first of Cranmer's Homilies emphasized the absolute centrality of regular Bible reading to the Christian life, and that his preface to the Great Bible had made the same point some years earlier; such an emphasis continued as he built the whole prayer book. Indeed, the preface to the completed book focused on this point almost to the exclusion of others:

> For [the church Fathers] so ordered the matter, that all the whole Bible (or the greatest part thereof) should be read over once in the year, intending thereby, that the Clergy, and specially such as were Ministers of the congregation, should (by often reading and meditation of God's word) be stirred up to godliness themselves, and be more able also to exhort others by wholesome doctrine, and to confute them that were adversaries to the truth. And further, that the people (by daily hearing of holy scripture read in the Church) should continually profit more and more in the knowledge of God, and be the more inflamed with the love of his true religion. But these many years passed this Godly and decent order of the ancient fathers, hath been so altered, broken, and neglected, by planting in un-

certain stories, Legends, Responds, Verses, vain repetitions, Commemorations, and Synodals, that commonly when any book of the Bible was began: before three or four Chapters were read out, all the rest were unread.[11]

In addition to having the congregation get through the whole Bible ("or the greatest part thereof") in a year, Cranmer wanted particular attention given to the Psalms, so often referred to as "the prayer book of the Bible" itself; his Kalendar outlined a schedule by which all 150 Psalms would be read each month. For Cranmer, regularization of the actual liturgy was important, but thorough knowledge of the Bible—by which alone people could be "stirred up to godliness" and enabled to "confute them that were adversaries to the truth"—was more important still.

Indeed, one could argue that Cranmer's chief reason for implementing standard liturgies was to provide a venue in which the Bible could be more widely and more thoroughly known. Each service would require the reading of several biblical passages. In the service of Holy Communion there were (and indeed are) typically four: an Old Testament passage, a Psalm, a passage from some part of the New Testament other than the Gospels, and a Gospel reading—all this in addition to the many sentences and phrases from Scripture woven into the liturgical language.

So the work continued, with Cranmer setting the direction and doing much of the compiling—working again in his great library at Croydon, as he had done when composing the Litany in 1544—and dealing with varying degrees of assistance and resistance from his fellow churchmen. The whole project is so closely associated with Cranmer, and was so clearly driven by him, that it is sometimes hard to discern the presence of the supporting cast. But it was there.

The Litany had long since been completed; the Homilies—which were not part of the prayer book itself but which provided key theological and pastoral context for it—written and distributed, the order for Communion promulgated and mandated, and the Kalendar worked out. A great deal remained to be done, but among that work some of the most important of all: the creation of rites for Morning and Evening Prayer, or, as they were commonly known, Matins and Evensong.

We have already noted the *horae canonicae*, the "canonical hours" of the monastic life, and the Daily Office containing the prayers for each "hour." The origins of these rites are lost, but they are closely associated with the vigil that the disciples of Jesus failed to keep when he was undergoing his agony in the Garden of Gethsemane. Most of his followers had abandoned him, and the few who remained snoozed as he prayed, thus earning his rebuke: "What, could ye not watch with me one hour?" (Matthew 26:40); after this they soon dozed off again. The regular prayers of monks and nuns are best understood as attempts by the church to assign some of its members to do what the disciples could not do: to stay awake and pray with the Lord. There is therefore a close link between the monastic hours and the sufferings of Good Friday. In their ideal form, as established by St. Benedict of Nursia in the sixth century, they are conducted every three hours and are named as follows: Matins (midnight); Lauds (3 a.m., or, more commonly, dawn); Prime (6 a.m.); Terce (9 a.m.); Sext (noon); Nones (3 p.m.); Vespers (6 p.m.); Compline (9 p.m.)

But the ideal may be unreachable: few human beings can thrive, or even survive, when getting no more than two uninterrupted hours of sleep each night. The needs of the body cannot simply be overridden even by the most willing spirit. Consequently, most monasteries and convents have either distributed the responsibility for keeping the hours among various members of the community, so that, for instance, those who say Matins are excused from Lauds, or have combined the hours in various ways, so that Vespers and Compline are said together before the community's bedtime, and Matins, Lauds, and Prime said immediately after rising.

But for Cranmer—who, it must be remembered, collaborated with Henry in the dissolution of England's monasteries—the whole system was deeply suspect however it happened to be tweaked. How can some members of Christ's Church be given the task of praying on behalf of the others? Are not all Christians commanded to pray, indeed to "pray without ceasing" (1 Thessalonians 5:17)? In this light, one of the greatest challenges of creating a prayer book for English Christians was to find a way to enable ordinary people who had their own daily work also to pray faithfully, to keep in their own way the vigil the first disciples had failed to keep.

Matins and Evensong were Cranmer's solution to this problem. Together, they constitute a brilliant solution indeed, and one of Cranmer's most lasting achievements, as later chapters of this history will show. Although many of the most heated, indeed poisonous, theological debates of the Reformation era concerned the events of the Mass—or the Holy Communion, or the Lord's Supper; the name of the rite was itself a major point of contention—the Anglicanism that developed from the *Book of Common Prayer* would be centered on the regular enactment, by millions of laypersons, of these simplified forms of the ancient Daily Office. Cranmer wished English Christians to take Communion more often than they had been accustomed to, yet as things turned out, weekly Communion did not become commonplace in the Church of England until the Victorian era. The typical parish Sunday service would contain Morning Prayer, perhaps followed by the Ante-Communion, that is, the parts of the Communion service preceding the administering of the Sacrament itself: prayers, the reading of the Decalogue, the recitation of the Creed, a sermon, and prayers for the church. At the end of the day, people would return for Evensong.[12]

So days were begun and ended in communal prayer. In institutions that featured chapel services—the colleges of Oxford and Cambridge most famously, but also public schools, preparatory schools, the Inns of Court—and where attendance was mandatory, this rhythm of worship was still more pronounced. Cranmer's 1549 order, which would later undergo significant change, begins with the priest reciting the Lord's Prayer "with a loud voice"—this in contrast to the old Roman practice, which likewise began Matins with the Lord's Prayer but instructed the priest to say it silently. After centuries of liturgical prayers being muttered in low tones, and in a language unknown to the people, the new model demands audible English. After this prayer comes a beautiful exchange taken from Psalm 51: the priest says, "O Lord, open thou my lips," and the people reply, "And my mouth shall shew forth thy praise." Then "O God, make speed to save me" calls forth the answer, "O Lord, make haste to help me." Such echoes and alternations are intrinsic to the structure of liturgical prayer: praise and petition, gratitude and need. The whole of the Matins service repeatedly enacts this oscillation.

After further prayers and readings from Scripture, the service comes to a close with a series of "collects" (pronounced with the emphasis on the first syllable):

these brief but highly condensed prayers were a specialty of Cranmer's. He did not invent them—Latin liturgies are full of them—but he gave them a distinctive English style that would be much imitated in the coming centuries. Here is the final collect of Matins:

> O LORD our heavenly father, almighty and everliving God, which hast safely brought us to the beginning of this day: defend us in the same with thy mighty power; and grant that this day we fall into no sin, neither run into any kind of danger, but that all our doings may be ordered by thy governance, to do always that is righteous in thy sight: through Jesus Christ our lord. Amen.[13]

Here we see the rhetorical structure common to most collects: a salutation to God; an acknowledgment of some core truth, in this case that the people come to prayer only because God has "safely brought us to the beginning of this day"; a petition ("grant us this day we fall into no sin"); an aspiration, or hope and purpose for the prayer, often introduced by the word "that" ("that all our doings may be ordered by thy governance"); and a concluding appeal to Jesus Christ as the mediator and advocate for God's people. Anglican liturgies are studded with these collects, many of them either composed fresh by Cranmer or adapted by him from Latin sources. They are among the most characteristic and recognizable features of prayer-book worship.

For the people of the sixteenth century, this thanksgiving for safe passage to a new day would not have been a merely pro forma acknowledgment. As A. Roger Ekirch has shown in his extraordinary history *At Day's Close: Night in Times Past*, the early modern period in England was marked by deep anxiety about the dangers of the nighttime world. With only limited forms of artificial lighting, people found the darkness continually befuddling: friend could not be distinguished from foe, nor animate objects from inanimate ones. The moon was thought to bring both madness and disease, and the night air was perceived as unhealthy, even poisonous. Ekirch quotes one woman whose thoughts were typical of the period: "At night, I pray Almighty God to keep me from ye power of evil spirits, and of evil men; from fearfull dreams and terrifying imaginations; from fire, and all sad accidents . . . so many mischiefs, I know of, doubtless more that I know not of."[14] *Doubtless more that I know not of*: the "Terrors of the Night," as Thomas Nashe called them in a 1594 pamphlet, multiplied relentlessly in the mind.

This was the context in which people came to Matins thanking the God "which hast safely brought us to the beginning of this day," and the context that determines the sober mood of Evensong. One can easily imagine the felt need to come together in church, before the fall of night, to beg God's protection, and indeed Evensong, which begins with a shortened version of the exchange that opens

Matins—"O God, make speed to save me"; "O Lord, make haste to help me"—concludes with a collect frankly admitting the fear of the dark, in a prayer so urgent that it even forgoes the customary decorous address to God and rushes straight to its petition: "Lighten our darkness we beseech thee, O Lord, & by thy great mercy defend us from all perils and dangers of this night, for the love of thy only son, our savior Jesu Christ. Amen."[15]

If each sunset brought its share of fears, the beginning and the end of life were more terrible still. The arrival of a child was cause for rejoicing, but in a period when approximately one in four children died before their first birthday,[16] that rejoicing was tempered by anxiety—an anxiety deepened by the belief that children were born under the curse of original sin and could only be rescued from that curse by the baptismal waters. Women who feared that their children would be stillborn even pleaded with priests to baptize those still in the womb, pouring the sanctified water over swollen bellies, lest the child suffer death and damnation before emerging into the world.[17] The prayer book's liturgy for Baptism does little to assuage such fears, beginning as it does with these sober words from the priest:

> Dear beloved, forasmuch as all men be conceived and born in sin, and that no man born in sin, can

enter into the kingdom of God (except he be regenerate, and born anew of water, and the holy ghost) I beseech you to call upon God the father through our Lord Jesus Christ, that of his bounteous mercy he will grant to these children that thing, which by nature they cannot have, that is to say, they may be baptized with the holy ghost, and received into Christ's holy Church, and be made lively members of the same.[18]

This is soon followed by an exorcism, performed under the assumption that infants come into this world not only corrupted by sin but also possessed by devils: "I command thee, unclean spirit, in the name of the father, of the son, and of the holy ghost, that thou come out, and depart from these infants." Under these sober circumstances, it had to have been an enormous relief to the parents to see their baptized and exorcised child clothed in a white baptismal gown and told, "Take this white vesture for a token of the innocency, which by God's grace in this holy sacrament of Baptism, is given unto thee."

Like life's beginning, its end, or possible end, was often full of fears, and here too the prayer book liturgies strike a curious balance between speaking, even exacerbating, those fears and pronouncing words of comfort. The rite for "The Visitation of the Sick" begins with a generous and confident plea in this collect:

O Lord look down from heaven, behold, visit, and relieve this thy servant: Look upon him with the eyes of thy mercy, give him comfort, and sure confidence in thee: Defend him from the danger of the enemy, and keep him in perpetual peace, and safety: through Jesus Christ our Lord. Amen.[19]

But this is soon followed by a reminder that the sick person needs to repent while he or she still can: "I require you to examine yourself, and your state, both toward God and man, so that accusing and condemning yourself for your own faults, you may find mercy at our heavenly father's hand, for Christ's sake, and not be accused and condemned in that fearful judgement."

For anyone accustomed to traditional Catholic practices, these liturgies are most noteworthy for what they lack: the saints, the blessed departed, the whole panoply of ritual and invocation that connects those now alive on earth with those now alive in the presence of God—or suffering the pains of Purgatory. (The damned are eternally and absolutely cut off from the rest of Creation; they cannot be addressed.) This absence is particularly striking in the rite for the sick, because it would ordinarily be at such times that people would call with special urgency on the saints, begging their intercession. We must remember in this context how Cranmer dealt with the dying King Henry: no prayers to the saints, no anointing with oil, no rite of extreme unction, none of the liturgical spectacle that had accompanied generations of Christians through their last moments; rather, just a simple request that the king somehow indicate his trust in Jesus Christ.

The historian Peter Brown has pointed out that the cult of the saints arose in a Roman culture in which ordinary people could do little to remedy any injustice they might suffer, or to clear themselves of any charges of wrongdoing. They needed friends in high places. If a local patrician could befriend them, then they had a chance of receiving justice or at least escaping punishment. "It is this hope of amnesty," Brown writes, "that pushed the saint to the foreground as *patronus*. For patronage and friendship derived their appeal from a proven ability to render malleable seemingly inexorable processes, and to bridge with the warm breath of personal acquaintance the great distances of the late-Roman social world. In a world so sternly organized around sin and justice, *patrocinium* [patronage] and *amicitia* [friendship] provided a much-needed language of amnesty."[20] By the early modern period in Europe, little had changed in this regard: common folk still looked fearfully upon local and national authorities, and particularly treasured those who could potentially mediate between the small and the great. Thus the continual invocations of saints in medieval rites and festivals, invocations the *Book of Common Prayer* largely expunges from its pages and from the common religious life. Cranmer kept certain saints' days in the Kalendar—and in this respect was considerably more traditionalist than the Continental evangelicals—but wrote prayers for those days that strenuously avoid any implication that the saints could intercede for the living or that they might be prayed to for any reason. In Cranmer's collects the saints are merely exemplary figures, as dead as the statues and windows that portrayed them.

In the world of the prayer book, then, the individual Christian stands completely naked before God in a paradoxical setting of public intimacy. There are no powerful rites conducted by sacerdotal figures while people stand some distance away fingering prayer beads or gazing on images of saints whose intercession they crave. Instead, people gather in the church to speak to God, and to be spoken to by Him, in soberly straightforward (though often very beautiful) English. Again and again they are reminded that there is but one Mediator between God and man, Jesus Christ. None other matters; so none other is called upon. The one relevant fact is His verdict upon us, and it is by faith in Him alone that we gain mercy at the time of judgment. All who stand in the church are naked before Him together, exposed in public sight. And so they say, using the first-person singular but using it together, *O God, make speed to save me; O Lord, make haste to help me.*

📖

The obvious contrast to the penitential tone of the rite for visiting the sick is the joyful marriage liturgy, The Form of Solemnization of Matrimony, the best-known rite in the prayer book. Phrases from it come easily to mind, and it need not be described in detail here. But the theology (and perhaps also the personal experience) underlying it should be noted.

The word "solemnization" does not perhaps sound joyous, but it is meant here to indicate that marriage is indeed a religious rite: not a civil contract, but a "holy estate" of life, as it is called in the opening pastoral discourse, which "Christ adorned and beautified with his presence, and first miracle that he wrought in Cana of Galilee." The rite is quite insistent on this point, and one cannot help suspecting that this is not just a repudiation of the common medieval belief that the chaste life of the "religious" (priest, monk, or nun) is intrinsically holier than the married life, though certainly Cranmer does mean to repudiate that idea. But also, Cranmer himself risked much by getting married, and did so twice. We know almost nothing about his first marriage, except that it occurred sometime between 1515 and 1519, that his wife's name was Joan, and that he had to resign his fellowship at Jesus College, Oxford, when he wed, leaving him to scrape for a living.

Joan died in childbirth, and their child died too, after which Jesus College offered to return his old fellowship. This led in turn to his being ordained as deacon and then as priest. As Diarmaid MacCulloch points out, if Joan had lived Cranmer would never have been ordained, and the difference that would have made to the English Reformation, and to any possible common-prayer book, is impossible to calculate though undoubtedly enormous. But she died, he was ordained, and by the time he married again—to the niece-by-marriage of a leading German Lutheran pastor—he was already Archbishop of Canterbury. We have noted his care to send his family away when Henry insisted on the absolute necessity of clerical celibacy, which may only indicate compassion, not marital devotion. But two small moments in the Rite for the Solemnization of Matrimony perhaps tell us a little more. As with all the prayer book's liturgies, this one draws on medieval forms: most of it simply translates the Sarum rite, which listed two primary justifications for marriage. First, marriage supports the procreation of children, and second, it is a "remedy against sin": as the bachelor St. Paul had written long before, "I say therefore to the unmarried and widows, it is good for them if they abide even as I. But if they cannot contain, let them marry: for it is better to marry than to burn" (1 Corinthians 7:8–9). But Cranmer added to these a third justification for marriage: "for the mutual society, help, and comfort, that the one ought to have of the other, both in prosperity and adversity."[21] Moreover, the Sarum order contained these words:

> I, [name], take thee, [name], to my wedded
> wife, to have and to hold from this day forward,
> for better, for worse, for richer, for poorer, in
> sickness, and in health, till death us depart: ac-

cording to God's holy ordinance: And thereto I plight thee my troth.

But to this existing form Cranmer added one more clause, one more obligation of the Christian husband to his wife, just before the mention of being parted by death: "to love and to cherish."[22]

And so the prayer book leads its readers from birth to sickness—sickness that might afflict the young as well as the old, which is why I treated it before the matrimonial rite—through marriage, and on to the inevitable end. Once death has come, the words of the prayer book are simply full of hope. The Order for the Burial of the Dead begins with these words from the Gospel of John: "I am the resurrection and the life (sayeth the Lord): he that believeth in me, yea though he were dead, yet shall he live. And whosoever liveth and believeth in me: shall not die for ever." And it ends with a sentence from the same Gospel, said also by Jesus: "And I will raise him up at the last day." This is an important closure, because the "last day"—the Day of Judgment, the *dies irae* or day of wrath—loomed large in the medieval imagination, and indeed often loomed quite literally above the worshippers, in wall paintings or "Judgment windows" where Christ, returned in glory, assigns to the unrepentant eternal misery and to the faithful eternal bliss. That note is sometimes struck in this burial liturgy,[23] but even those moments are woven together with sweet words of comfort:

Grant unto this thy servant, that the sins which he committed in this world be not imputed unto him, but that he, escaping the gates of hell and pains of eternal darkness: may ever dwell in the region of light, with Abraham, Isaac, and Jacob, in the place where is no weeping, sorrow, nor heaviness: and when that dreadful day of the general resurrection shall come, make him to rise also with the just and righteous, and receive this body again to glory, then made pure and incorruptible, set him on the right hand of thy son Jesus Christ, among thy holy and elect.[24]

Particularly important is the emphasis on the resurrection of the *body*: in a world where lives were, in comparison to those in much of the world today, so short, injury so difficult of treatment, and disease so irresistible, the belief that bodies of the faithful would be renewed in "glory," made "pure and incorruptible," was a central hope. If the emphasis of the baptismal liturgy was on the spiritual dangers into which children are born, and of the Visitation of the Sick on the urgent need for heartfelt repentance, the burial rite is focused consistently on the Resurrection of Jesus Christ as a pledge and guarantee of the resurrection and glorification of all believers.

There is much more in the book, but we have traced its foundation, which would remain largely in place through future revisions. The completed *Book of Common Prayer* considers time in three aspects. First, in its Kalendar, it treats salvation history, walking the people of God through the seasons of the church year, following the sequence of events from the Fall of humanity to the Second Coming and the Last Judgment. Second, it treats the passage of each human being through the stages of life, from birth to burial. And third, in the bookends of Matins and Evensong, it treats the diurnal rhythms of each given day. The prayer book masters and orders time on each of these scales; it renders temporal experience accessible and meaningful for each Christian participating in the life of Christ's Church. All this is contained in one book. Once Cranmer and his allies had made it, what remained was the promulgation of this book throughout the young king's realm; what remained was the enforcement of *uniformity*.

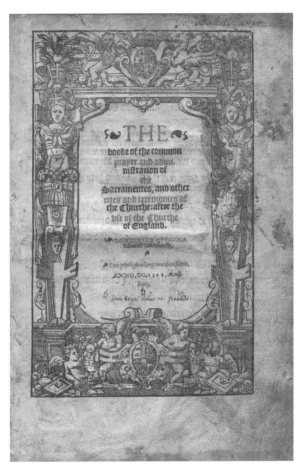

FIGURE 2. The title page of the first *Book of Common Prayer* (1549), as printed by the London printer Edward Whitchurch, who after the execution of Thomas Cranmer married the archbishop's widow.

Photograph courtesy of the Francis Donaldson Library at Nashotah House Theological Seminary.

Revision, Banishment, Restoration

CHAPTER 2

The employment of the *Book of Common Prayer* was made mandatory through England by the Act of Uniformity, passed by Parliament in early 1549. It declared

> that all and singular ministers in any cathedral or parish church or other place within this realm of England, Wales, Calais, and the marches of the same, or other the king's dominions, shall, from and after the feast of Pentecost next coming, be bound to say and use the Matins, Evensong, celebration of the Lord's Supper, commonly called the Mass, and administration of each of the sacraments, and all their common and open prayer, in such order and form as is mentioned in the same book, and none other or otherwise.[1]

Its passage was controversial. Among the eighteen bishops in the House of Lords during the debates over the act—which succeeded a series of theologically intense debates about the original authorization of the prayer book—eight ended up voting against it. These were largely traditionalist figures, but it should be noted that a particular person's theology can never be inferred simply from the fact of his or her opposition to a particular version of the Anglican prayer book. As Brian Cummings has commented, "in practice, the *Book of Common Prayer* seemed to please almost no one. Many Elizabethans were still Catholic at heart, and conformed only reluctantly to a church now bereft of spiritual comfort and external signs. Puritans, on the other hand, mocked even the use of the surplice; rejected the wafer in favor of ordinary bread; objected to the sign of the cross in Baptism, kneeling for Communion, the ring in marriage . . . and bowing at the name of Jesus."[2] To this theme we will repeatedly have cause to return.

Nevertheless, lordly opposition was overcome: Cranmer's *Book of Common Prayer* was approved, its uniform employment mandated ("none other or otherwise"), and sanctions for noncompliance specified. Indeed, of the 2,700 words comprising the act, more than 2,000 of them are devoted to the listing of offenses against the new book and the prescribing of punishments for any "obstinate person who willingly would disturb so godly order and quiet in this realm" by refusing to conform. Among ministers, repeat offenses could lead even to life imprisonment.[3] The first copies of the book appeared in early March and were quickly adopted by evangelical parishes, and at St. Paul's Cathedral. On the "feast of Pentecost," or Whitsunday, June 9, 1549, the *Book of Common Prayer* and the Act of Uniformity became the law of the king's whole realm. And then the troubles began.

Troubles arose in high places and low. The evangelical aristocrats who governed England had spies keeping a close eye on Mary, the king's older sister and a known Catholic. They reported that she ignored the new book and continued to have the old Latin Mass said for her just as it had always been said. Meanwhile, in the West country, riots broke out. The day after Whitsunday parishioners in Sampford Courtenay, Devon, demanded that their priest return to the old rite, and then decided to march to the nearest big town, Exeter, to make their complaints more public. As they marched they drew more and more supporters, and (according to Cranmer's theological ally Martin Bucer, who wrote a letter describing the rebellion) gathered up and burned every copy of the new prayer book they could find. They mocked the new liturgy as "but like a Christmas game" and demanded the restoration of the old Latin rite— complete with the elevation of the Host, which Cranmer had forbidden—and the Six Articles from Henry's time. Moreover, many of the rebels were Cornishmen who already felt themselves wrongly subjected to English authority: imposing the English language upon their traditional worship was rubbing salt into their wounds. "And so we the Cornish men (whereof certain of us understand no English) utterly refuse this new English." It was pointed out to them that they didn't understand Latin either, but in a sense they did: they understood that Latin was the language of a church that spread far beyond England and that heretofore had not been under English control. And if Latin was incomprehensible to them, it was equally incomprehensible to their English rulers. Nevertheless, their protests were silenced and the rebellion broken: as many as five thousand rebels were slaughtered.

Meanwhile, many of the more rigorous evangelicals—including some very close to the throne—found themselves dismayed by the remnants of traditional worship (what they called "papistry") in the prayer book. Cranmer may have retained the Litany he wrote for Henry in 1544, with its prayer for deliverance "from the tyranny of the bishop of Rome and all his detestable enormities," but in their view it would do no good to banish the pope only to repeat his worst crimes and errors. They saw that the priest, though he began Matins by speaking English "in a loud voice," did so from the choir of the church, while the people by implication remained in the nave. The rite thus continued the separation of the clergy and people that had been intrinsic to the old High Mass but was despised by the evangelicals, even in the context of a non-Eucharistic service, as promoting superstition. More worrisome still, this officiant was *called* "priest," rather than merely "minister": it is the function of a priest to preside at a sacrifice, and in the evangelical view, the Roman liturgy was profoundly heretical in its implication that Christ is sacrificed anew in each Mass. If there is no sacrifice, then what need for a priest? For the same reason the place on which the bread and wine were placed during the service should simply be called a "table," but the prayer book called it an "altar." Worst of all was Cranmer's name—or rather names: he seems here to have been trying to give something to everyone—for the central rite: "The Supper of the Lord and the Holy Communion, Commonly Called the Mass." Yes, replied the evangelicals, it is indeed "commonly called the Mass," but that is just what must be eliminated, lest people believe that this new rite is merely the familiar superstitious nonsense clothed in English rather than Latin. Especially for those evangelicals who knew the radical dismantling of old forms of worship carried out by reformers on the Continent, Cranmer's prayer book was maddeningly traditionalist, nearly papistical. (And those hardline evangelicals who disdained set prayers altogether—we shall hear more from them later—said it simply *was* papistical, and hence devilish.)

In one sense Cranmer and the government did not back down: the new book was not withdrawn, the Act of Uniformity was not repealed, and offenders against "godly order and quiet in this realm" were punished. Much of Cranmer's time in the second half of 1549 was devoted to supervising investigations of heresy, among the radical evangelicals and traditionalists alike. But revisions of the prayer book began almost immediately, and they all followed the direction the evangelical party preferred. Cranmer may not have been wholly dismayed by this turn of events. As noted earlier, his first experiments with English liturgies in the 1530s were far more radical than the 1549 book, and perhaps he only pushed that book as far as he thought he could go in the evangelical direction. This was certainly what he or some close allies told the Continental reformer Martin Bucer when he visited London that April. Bucer wrote to friends back home that the traditionalist elements in the prayer book "are only to be retained for a time, lest the people, not yet thoroughly instructed in Christ, should by too extensive innovations be frightened away from Christ's religion." Bucer clearly believed a simplified, pared-down order of worship to be the only appropriate kind—"Christ's religion"—and equally clearly he believed that Cranmer shared his views. Diarmaid MacCulloch, Cranmer's authoritative biographer, agrees with Bucer.[4]

But there are also reasons for thinking that Cranmer saw the 1549 book as striking a proper balance between traditionalism and reform. In April of 1552 a second Act of Uniformity was passed, though the book it demanded allegiance to was not yet finished. This act reads as though it were, as it surely was, written by an extremely peevish Archbishop of Canterbury. It praises the 1549 book as "agreeable to the Word of God and the primitive Church, very comfortable to all good people desiring to live in Christian conversation," and explains that a new book is needed not for "any worthy cause" but "because there has arisen in the use and exercise of the aforesaid common service in the Church, heretofore set forth, divers doubts for the fashion and manner of the ministrations of the same."[5] These do not seem the words or thoughts of someone delighted to go further toward the Continental models than he had gone before; they seem rather to suggest a deep annoyance at being forced, under political pressure, to make unnecessary and largely cosmetic changes. Arguments that Cranmer was dissatisfied by the 1549 book and was only truly happy with the 1552 revision are not based on his own words, but rather on what his colleagues and allies said and wrote. Martin Bucer certainly saw 1549 as a way station, and Hugh Latimer, perhaps Cranmer's closest confederate, was quite unhappy with the Romish residue in the book. But Cranmer's only recorded words on the subject are the ones cited above, which praise the 1549 book. He may have been speaking in politic terms, or he may have been content with a book whose rites could be interpreted in multiple ways and therefore, while not fully satisfactory to any one party, remained plastic enough to be put to use by all of them.

In any event, whether the 1552 revisions were cosmetic or substantive depends on one's theological point of view. Certainly the evangelicals felt they had won significant changes: not only were the words "Mass" and "altar" banished, but also the Communion liturgy was revised to remove certain ambiguities that might have allowed for a transubstantiationalist interpretation of the liturgical events. Matins was renamed Morning Prayer, Evensong became Evening Prayer, again in the cause of eliminating papistical echoes. (But the name *Evensong* would continue to be widely used, surely because of its beauty.) First-person-singular pronouns were often replaced by plural ones—*O God, make speed to save us; O Lord, make haste to help us*—presumably in order to emphasize further the communal nature of the liturgy and to discourage the devotional individualism that had been so common in the Middle Ages. Probably because many evangelicals perceived exorcism as a purely theatrical rite, and believed that priests taught people to fake signs of possession and then fake deliverance from their "demons," the exorcism was removed from the baptismal rite.[6]

But there were some points on which Cranmer simply would not budge. Almost uniquely among the leading Reformers of the age, he insisted on a Kalendar that followed the ancient pattern of the Church Year much as the Roman church kept it. And most controversially of all, he defended the practice of kneeling at Communion. For the more radical evangelicals—led by the uncompromising Scot John Knox—this was as bad as calling the Lord's table an altar, and the same issues were at stake. In the gestural vocabulary of the time, kneeling signified reverence before a great Lord; therefore, to kneel while receiving Communion was to proclaim that you believe that bread and wine are no longer present, having been transubstantiated into the body and blood of the Lord Christ. Cranmer seems to have found this argument ridiculous. He replied that such kneeling was a "thing being well meant, for a signification of the humble and grateful acknowledging of the benefits of Christ, given unto the worthy receiver, and to avoid the profanation and disorder, which about the holy Communion might else ensue"—that is, to kneel is simply to acknowledge the dignity and seriousness of the occasion. Knox demanded that Communion be taken while seated, but since he also claimed to draw all his principles directly from biblical precedent, Cranmer sardonically replied that if they wished to follow the apostolic model, then Communion should only be taken while reclining on one arm, since that was first-century Palestinian custom, "like Tartars and Turks today."[7]

Neither party would yield on this matter. The impasse was serious, because the evangelicals had the parliamentary power to prevent the revised prayer book from being issued until it met their requirements. Disputation extended through the summer and into the autumn, until finally a compromise was reached. Knox and his fellow radicals would grudgingly permit kneeling, but only if Cranmer were to write, and insert into the book, a kind of disclaimer. It began with the insistence on the legitimacy of the practice quoted above, and then continued:

Lest the same kneeling might be thought or taken otherwise, we do declare that it is not meant thereby, that any adoration is done, or ought to be done, either unto the Sacramental bread or wine there bodily received, or unto any real and essential presence there being of Christ's natural flesh and blood. For as concerning the sacramental bread and wine, they remain still in their very natural substances, and therefore may not be adored, for that were Idolatry to be abhorred of all faithful Christians. And as concerning the natural body and blood of our Saviour Christ, they are in heaven and not here.[8]

This is palpably crabby. The first printing of the new book had already come off the presses, so this disclaimer had to be printed separately and inserted into the existing books. Such liturgical instructions are called rubrics, and were typically printed in red ink, but regular ink was used in this case, so it came to be known as the Black Rubric. It resolved the dispute for the moment, but the underlying issues continued to simmer and would boil over again and again.

Still, Cranmer and his allies must have been pleased at what they had accomplished. They had now produced a *Book of Common Prayer* that retained some of the most venerable and beautiful aspects of traditional worship but also fully embodied the evangelical commitment to serious engagement with Scripture, and offered a communal liturgical enactment of what it means to live in faith and by grace. Traditionalists were unhappy, but their numbers and their power were decreasing; and the people would soon become used to the new forms of worship, and would be, as Bucer put it, "thoroughly instructed in Christ."

And then King Edward died.

📖

The young king had been sickly for some time, so his death was not unexpected, and the evangelical lords who ran the country, chief among them the Duke of Northumberland, had already formulated plans for retaining power despite the obvious and deeply troubling fact that the clear legal heir to the throne was Edward's Catholic sister, Mary: the Third Succession Act of 1544 had specifically placed Mary and the younger sister, Elizabeth, in direct line of succession. Seeking to avoid the inevitable—not just because the law spoke so unambiguously but because continued unrest throughout the kingdom revealed how shaky the evangelicals' hold on power was—Northumberland got the dying Edward to name his sixteen-year-old cousin, Lady Jane Grey, as his heir, which led only to the well-known tragic farce of her coronation, deposition, and ultimate execution.

King Edward died on July 6, 1553; Jane was proclaimed queen three days later. On the fourteenth, Northumberland led troops from London to confront Mary and her supporters in East Anglia, but his absence merely allowed the Privy Council the opportunity to switch allegiances, which they did, throwing their support to Mary on the nineteenth and imprisoning Lady Jane. On August 3, Mary rode triumphantly into London; later that month Northumberland was executed, and in September Parliament confirmed Mary's status as the rightful queen of the realm.

Although many leading evangelicals fled the country at this time, Thomas Cranmer, perhaps surprisingly, did not. Edward's state funeral, in Westminster Abbey, was not held until August 8, after Mary had assumed the throne. Cranmer presided over it, using the rites from his own prayer book. He had been intimately involved in the proclamation of Lady Jane as queen, and had even sent men to fight with Northumberland; he could not have hoped to escape imprisonment, yet he remained. In the end he became the most famous martyr of the English Reformation: after imprisonment, interrogation, torture, dismissal from the priesthood, a coerced recantation of his evangelical belief, and a very dramatic last-minute public recantation of that recantation, he was burned to death in the middle of Oxford's Broad Street on March 20, 1556.[9]

In a significant and touching turn of events, care for Cranmer's family fell to the evangelical publishers and booksellers of London, most prominent among them Edward Whitchurch, who had been one of the first two authorized printers of the *Book of Common Prayer*. Whitchurch married Cranmer's widow, Margaret, smuggled his son to the Continent, and arranged a marriage for his daughter. But he could not save the books that Cranmer had created and he had printed.

One of Mary's first acts as queen was to oversee the repeal of the Act of Uniformity and the de-authorization of the *Book of Common Prayer*. (The 1552 book, so passionately disputed in its making, ended up lasting about six months.) By her authority the old Sarum rite was restored, along with the saints to their accustomed places, and the whole rich apparatus of late medieval Christianity. The prayer books that survived went with their owners to the Continent, where they helped to sustain communities of English evangelicals in exile. Mary's men searched out evangelical heretics throughout the land as eagerly as Cranmer had searched out traditionalist ones just a few years earlier. This might have been the end of Cranmer's great liturgical experiment, except that Mary's time on the throne was even shorter than her brother's: she died on November 17, 1558, leaving her throne to her sister, Elizabeth. And Elizabeth's sympathies were with the evangelical party, and with Cranmer's book.

📖

That there would be no continuation of Mary's policies became absolutely and publicly clear at Elizabeth's coronation. Elizabeth entered Westminster

Abbey accompanied by a choir singing the Litany—in English.[10] The Communion service was also in English, and the sacramental bread was conspicuously *not* elevated. However, as it soon proved, the Cranmerian book with which the new Queen was more sympathetic was the first one: the relatively traditionalist book of 1549. She was an evangelical, but a moderate one, and willing to tolerate a good deal more of the time-honored practices than many of her advisers. (Some of the evangelical ministers who tended her were continually dismayed by her preference for adornments to churches and chapels, including far more candles than they thought either righteous or seemly.) Ultimately, those advisers, led by the shrewd William Cecil, convinced her that the 1552 book was the more politic choice, but, perhaps at her insistence, some reversions to the earlier text were implemented. The Black Rubric, which Cranmer had so grudgingly written, was deleted, and the ambiguous language in the 1549 Communion rite was restored—a matter of great consequence, since it allowed worshippers to believe that Christ was in some way, not specifically defined, truly present in the bread and wine. This was crucial to traditionalist acceptance of the rite, both at that moment and later in Anglican history. It is noteworthy that the Elizabethan book also deleted the Litany's reference to the "detestable enormities" of the pope.

Thanks to Elizabeth's long reign—forty-five years—it was this 1559 *Book of Common Prayer* that did more than any other to consolidate the distinctively Anglican form of worship. Eamon Duffy, near the end of his magisterial celebration of the medieval piety that prayer-book worship displaced, acknowledges, in a melancholy tone, the power the prayer book came to exert in the lives of English Christians. "The conformity of the majority [to the Elizabethan settlement] did not mean the end of traditional religion. Instead, slowly, falteringly, much reduced in scope, depth, and coherence, it re-formed itself around the rituals and words of the prayer-book." Thanks to the relative stability of the Elizabethan era, the *Book of Common Prayer* was given decades to settle into people's lives, to replace the old rites and practices—not, perhaps, in ways that Duffy finds adequate to compensate for what was lost, but nonetheless. "Cranmer's sombrely magnificent prose, read week by week, entered and possessed their minds, and became the fabric of their prayer, the utterance of their most solemn and their most vulnerable moments."[11]

¶ And there ſhalbe no celebration of the loꝛdes ſupper, except there be a good number to Communicate wyth the Pꝛieſt, accoꝛdyng to hys diſcretion.

¶ And if there be not aboue .rr. perſons in the Paryſh, of diſcretion to receiue the Communion, yet there ſhalbe no communion except foure oꝛ thꝛe at the leaſt comunicate wyth the pꝛieſt. And in Cathedꝛal, & collegiate churches, where be many Pꝛieſtes & Deacons, they ſhal all receyue the communion wyth the miniſter euery Sondap at the leaſt, except they haue a reaſonable cauſe to the contrary.

¶ Although no oꝛder can be ſo perfitly deuiſed, but it may be of ſome eyther foꝛ theyꝛ ignoꝛaunce and infyꝛmity, oꝛ els of malice & obſtinacy miſconſtrued, depꝛaued, & interpꝛeted in a wꝛong part, and yet becauſe bꝛotherly charitye willeth, that ſo much as couenientty may be, Offences ſhould be taken away, therfoꝛe we willing to do the ſame. Wheras it is oꝛdeyned in the boke of comune pꝛayer, in thadminiſtration of the Loꝛdes Supper, that the communicantes kneling, ſhould receyue the holy comunion, whych thyng beyng wel ment foꝛ a ſignification of the humble & gratefull acknowledgyng of the benefites of Chꝛiſt, geue vnto the woꝛthy receyuer, & to auoide the pꝛophanation, & diſoꝛder whyche about the holy comunion myght els enſue, leſt yet the ſame kneling myght bethought oꝛ take otherwiſe, we do declare that it is not ment therby that any adoꝛation is done, oꝛ ought to be done either vnto the ſacramétal bꝛead oꝛ wine, ther bodely receiued, oꝛ vnto ani real, & eſſential pꝛeſence ther beyng, of Chꝛiſtes natural fleſh & bloud. Foꝛ as côcerning the ſacramétal bꝛead & wine, they remaine ſtil in their very natural ſubſtaûces, & therfoꝛe may not be adoꝛed, foꝛ that wer idolatry, to be abhoꝛred of al faythful chꝛiſtiens, & as concerninge the natural boꝛdy and bloud of our ſauiour Chꝛiſt, they are in heauen, & not here, foꝛ it is agaynſt the truthe of Chꝛiſtes true natural body, to be in mo places then in one at one tyme.

¶ And to take awaye the ſuperſtition, whyche anye perſon hath, oꝛ myghte haue in the bꝛeade and wine, it ſhall ſuffice that the bꝛeade be ſuch as is vſual to be eaté at the table, with other meates, but the beſt and pureſt wheate bꝛead, that couentently may be gotten. And if anye of the bꝛead oꝛ wyne remaine, the Curate ſhal haue it to his owne vſe,

¶ The bread and wyne foꝛ the communion ſhalbe pꝛouided by the Curate and the church wardeines, at the charges of the Paryſhe, and the Paryſhe ſhalbe diſcharged of ſuche ſummes of money, oꝛ other duties, which hitherto they haue payed foꝛ the ſame by oꝛder of their houſes

Becoming Venerable

The "sombrely magnificent prose" of the prayer book remains its single most striking feature. It is highly rhythmical and consistently reliant on Latinate structures, but it borrows from biblical Hebrew a deep allegiance to parallelism. Some of Cranmer's most memorable phrases involve doublings, often alliterative: we have already noted the twin alliterations of "make speed to save us" and "make haste to help us," but there are many more, and almost every imaginable way to present parallel clauses either for reinforcement or for contrast. Consider—as one example among many possible—the "general confession" of sin that first appeared in the Morning Prayer rite of the 1552 book:

> Almighty and most merciful father, we have
> erred and strayed from thy ways, like lost sheep.
> We have followed too much the devices and de-
> sires of our own hearts. We have offended against
> thy holy laws. We have left undone those things

which we ought to have done, and we have done those things which we ought not to have done, and there is no health in us: but thou, O Lord, have mercy upon us miserable offenders. Spare thou them, O God, which confess their faults. Restore thou them that be penitent, according to thy promises declared unto mankind, in Christ Jesus our Lord. And grant, O most merciful father, for his sake, that we may hereafter live a godly, righteous, and sober life, to the glory of thy holy name. Amen.[1]

This is rhetorically masterful in multiple ways. Alliteration we have, of course—"devices and desires"—and other doublings, as in "erred and strayed."[2] Cranmer employs the additive power of parataxis, linking clauses by simple conjunction: "We have left undone those things which we ought to have done, *and* we have done those things which we ought not to have done, *and* there is no health in us." The prayer begins and ends with invocations to God as "most merciful father," which is appropriate given that this is a plea for mercy, forgiveness. (Those praying also refer to themselves as "miserable offenders," which modern ears do not like, but "miserable"—from the Latin *miserere*—means simply "in need of mercy.") Perhaps most striking of all is what Cranmer does with the grammatical subjects of his clauses: "*We* have erred and strayed . . . *We* have followed . . . *We* have offended . . . *We* have left undone . . . *we* have done"—

this pronoun ringing like a bell—and then the sudden pivot: "but *thou*, O Lord, have mercy . . . spare *thou* . . . restore *thou*." Note also the chiasmus of putting the subject before the verb when describing our actions and after it when describing the hoped-for actions of God, which creates a mirroring effect: our miserable offending counterbalanced by the mercy of the righteous Lord.

Almost every page of the *Book of Common Prayer* contains just such a miniature textbook of rhetorical effects, typically executed with virtuosity. It was C. S. Lewis's belief that the virtuosity arises from the need to adapt Latin devotional language to the very different character of English: Latin translated over-literally tends to be precious and pompous, and Cranmer was determined to avoid those traps. The Latin originals were "almost over-ripe in their artistry"; the English of the prayer book "arrests them, binds them in strong syllables, strengthens them even by limitations, as they in return erect and transfigure it. Out of that conflict the perfection springs."[3] It is especially instructive, then, to study Cranmer's sources in order to see how he adds to or deviates from them in order to produce these effects, almost all of which take on a greater power when said aloud, and still more when said aloud by a whole congregation. For it was surely congregational worship that Cranmer had primarily in mind when shaping the words of this book: his English is meant to find its fullest life when said aloud, in unison, the *vox populi* made the organ on which this verbal music shall be played.

Yet he was mindful of private devotional needs as well. We have already noted now the prayer book replaced a motley collection of liturgical manuals employed by priests and other participants in public rites, but it is also, and perhaps equally, the successor of some of the most widely used manuals of personal devotion from the Middle Ages: the primers, or books of hours. Generally speaking, these books are called primers when in vernacular languages, books of hours (or *horae*) when in Latin, but their content was quite similar. Such books typically contained the Psalms, readings from the Gospels, prayers from the Daily Office, and a series of personal, often-penitential prayers, at least some of them directed to Mary. Often they are illuminated—that is, illustrated, sometimes lavishly: some of the most beautiful books of the Middle Ages are *horae*, for instance, the famous *Très Riches Heures du duc de Berry*. Some of them are rather large—the pages of the Duc de Berry's book were probably, in their original form, about the size of a piece of modern legal paper—but others were tiny, meant for the pocket or reticule. Lady Jane Grey carried with her to her execution a book smaller than 3 inches high, partially illuminated and filled with English prayers written in Gothic letters by a professional scribe, to which she had added her own prayerful commentary. (Aside from the obvious historical interest of such a book, it also reveals that the coming of the printing press had not simply ended the old traditions of scribal writing and book making.)

The preface of the 1549 *Book of Common Prayer* notes that "by this order, the curates shall need none other books for their public service, but this book and the Bible: by the means whereof, the people shall not be at so great charge for books, as in time past they have been."[4] That is, Cranmer hoped that ordinary parishioners—those who were literate, at any rate—would be able to afford their own copies of the prayer book, which, along with the Bible that Cranmer so earnestly exhorts laypersons to read, would equip them fully for the basic practices of the Christian life. Presumably at Cranmer's encouragement, King Edward issued a royal decree capping the price of prayer books: three shillings eightpence bound, or two shillings twopence for the leaves alone, for those who wished to have the book bound according to their particular preferences.[5]

Many copies of the early editions of the *Book of Common Prayer* survive in a variety of sizes. The largest ones are folios—approximately 12 by 15 inches—and these were clearly meant for parish use, to be read from in public worship by priests. The smallest are 64mo (or sexagesimo-quarto, 1/32 the size of a folio), as is Lady Jane's book. The print in the 64mo books is so tiny as to be unreadable for all but the most nearsighted, which arouses the suspicion that the books were kept as talismans rather than used as devotional manuals. This would of course have outraged Cranmer, but such uses were perhaps inevitable in a culture accustomed to being in the presence of a wide range of holy objects—crucifixes, relics, highly painted statues, sacramental furniture of various kinds, holy water, and above all the transfigured Bread and Wine—most of which Cranmer and his fellow evangelicals had taken away from them. The holiest objects remaining in the world shaped by the stricter evangelicals were books; it was inevitable that some would treat them as they had always treated holy things, with reverence bordering on (or indistinguishable from) superstition.

But thousands of English Christians read their prayer books and used them faithfully for private as well as public worship. The same cadences they whispered to themselves when alone, or read silently, or read aloud in the presence of their household, also accompanied them to church. It was therefore through public rites and private devotions alike that the book's language "entered and possessed their minds." The beauty of that language, together with its great debts to more ancient forms of worship— Lewis rightly notes that Cranmer and the other makers of the prayer book "wished their book to be praised not for original genius but for catholicity and antiquity"—made the book venerable in but a few generations. When later political troubles deprived English Christians of their prayer books, they felt as bereft as their ancestors had when the old Latin Mass was taken from them.

📖

If in the mid-sixteenth century the chief threats to the success of the prayer book had come from traditionalists who wanted the medieval rites and practices restored, a century later the threat came from the opposite end of the theological spectrum. Indeed, that balance had shifted even before the end of Elizabeth's reign. Richard Hooker, the greatest of Anglican theologians, writing at the end of the sixteenth century, devoted a great deal of his massive *Laws of Ecclesiastical Polity* to a defense of the prayer book against Puritans who preferred a mode of worship purged of *all* popish residue—and for some of them this could only be accomplished by completely eliminating set forms of prayer.[6] Before saying anything about the prayer book itself, Hooker patiently works through the evidence that, to his mind, clearly shows that both ancient Jews and Christians of the apostolic era employed set prayers. "If prayers were no otherwise accepted of God than being conceived always new, according to the exigence of present occasions; if it be right to judge him by our own bellies, and to imagine that he doth loathe to have the selfsame supplications often iterated, even as we do to be every day fed without alteration or change of diet; if prayers be actions which ought to waste away themselves in the making; if being made to remain that they may be resumed and used again as prayers, they be but instruments of superstition"; but these assumptions, says Hooker, are obviously absurd. And did not Christ himself institute a form of prayer—the Lord's Prayer—that almost all Christians employ in their worship?[7]

Half a century later, one of the most powerful opponents of the *Book of Common Prayer* would not grant even that point: John Milton's *Eikonoklastes* (1649) is a pamphlet whose chief subject is the rightness of throwing off tyranny, which can be political (as in the case of King Charles I, whose execution Milton defends) but also spiritual. And Milton does not scruple to say that set prayers, or as he terms them, the "servile yoke of liturgy," are tyrannical: "to imprison and confine by force, into a pinfold of set words, those two most unimprisonable things, our prayers, and that divine spirit of utterance that moves them, is a tyranny that would have longer hands than those giants who threatened bondage to heaven." As for the Lord's Prayer: "Why was neither that prayer, nor any other set form, ever after used, or so much as mentioned by the apostles, much less commended to our use?" And if we are not to use the Lord's Prayer, "Much less can it be lawful that an Englished massbook, composed, for ought we know, by men neither learned, nor godly, should justle out, or at any time deprive us the exercise of that heavenly gift, which God by special promise pours out daily upon his church, that is to say, the spirit of prayer."[8] It was necessary, then, to throw off all forms of tyranny at once: the despotism of the king and the despotism of the book. For some Puritans, the prayer book was even worse than tyrannical, it was Satanic. Matthew Hopkins, who in the 1640s claimed to hold the office of Witchfinder General, solemnly proclaimed that when the Devil performed the marriages of witches he invariably used the matrimonial rite from the prayer book.[9]

To understand these views, and how they led to a second banishment of the *Book of Common Prayer*, one might begin with the Millenary Petition of 1603. In this petition, given to King James VI of Scotland, as after Elizabeth's death he traveled south to London, where he would be crowned as her successor on the English throne, as many as a thousand Puritan ministers summed up their frustrations with the existing prayer book and their demands for change. At the very least they wanted elimination of anything in the book that smelled of Rome—the use of the terms "priest" and "altar," the suggestion that ministers are empowered even to pronounce (much less to grant) absolution from sin, the use of special clerical costume, the making of the sign of the cross at baptism, and the like—but for many these changes would mark just a way station toward the abolition of the prayer book and, further, of the whole episcopal system of church governance. And of course episcopacy in England had become deeply interwoven with royal power, which led to the rallying cry of the most reckless Puritans: "No Bishop, No King!"

James, perhaps wanting to show himself a reasonable and open-minded sovereign, or perhaps just motivated by his immoderate love of disputation, immediately convened a meeting with church leaders of varying camps to consider the Millenary Petition. The Hampton Court Conference of January 1604 is now most famous for having resulted in the commissioning of a new translation of the Bible, which was completed in 1611 and was authorized for use throughout the realm, and experienced, one might say, a certain degree of success. But in the context of the period, what matters more is James's decision to meet only a few of the Puritans' demands. The prayer book itself underwent only very minor revisions. Puritan frustration at the direction the Church of England was taking was thus only temporarily lessened, and in the coming decades that frustration would return and grow, especially after William Laud became Archbishop of Canterbury in 1633. Laud was a committed supporter of traditional religious forms and practices—what came to be known as "high-church" religion, as opposed to the "low-church" preferences of the Puritans and the "broad-church" or "latitudinarian" model that would become increasingly influential in the later seventeenth century—and of royal prerogatives over against those of Parliament.[10] Nor was Laud shy about enforcing his beliefs. It became increasingly clear in Laud's first years of power that King and Parliament were headed for a terrible confrontation, and that the *Book of Common Prayer* was firmly linked with increasingly unpopular bishops and an increasingly unstable royal presence. When the king finally fell, so too did the prayer book.

Here again the story can only be told briefly, and in a way that demonstrates the curious entanglement of the prayer book with other—or seemingly other—forces: it has often been the victim, and occasionally the beneficiary, of its associations. Throughout the early modern period in England, the prayer book was accompanied by a particular model of church governance, and, more explosively still, a particular model of the relations between church and state. Some of these entanglements are historically accidental, but many were inevitable because of the peculiar nature of this book: not just a set of prayers but also a set of *instructions*—recipes, as it were, for liturgical actions, actions that placed people in relation to objects in the world. This was evident in the contentiousness of the 1552 debates on the posture appropriate to receiving communion: against John Knox, Cranmer fought merely to *permit* kneeling, though those whose consciences resisted the symbolic implications of that posture were allowed to stand. But eighty years later Archbishop Laud would have a stricter understanding of conformity and uniformity; so, to the outrage of Puritans and evangelicals, he reinterpreted the rubrics in the prayer book and made kneeling a condition of reception. (To facilitate this, and to keep people from desecrating the altar area, Laud ordered communion rails installed in churches; these later became especially hated because of their association with compulsion, and when Laud fell they were ripped out of churches all over England and gleefully burned in great bonfires.)

Moreover, if one is to take Communion in both kinds, as the rubrics specified, one must drink from a vessel, and vessels signify. For this reason the Cranmerian church had gathered and melted down the elaborate and beautiful chalices and patens of the medieval church, replacing them with simple drinking cups. Laud tossed those out and commissioned chalices made on medieval patterns. In these and other ways evangelicals were made to feel coerced toward papistry in their own parish churches, even though Laud thoroughly disdained the Roman church.[11] All of these conflicts stemmed from the legally mandated authority of a book that gave instruction for the performance of highly meaningful acts. This peculiarity made the prayer book, in turbulent times especially, a nearly unique focus of disputation. Only the Bible could excel it in this regard, and just barely.

For most of his reign King James shrewdly balanced the competing claims of the Puritans and the high-church party, and even spoke of the need for reunion with Catholics, but in his last years the high-church party became dominant—largely through the work of their leading advocate at court, the king's favorite the Duke of Buckingham—and their sway over James's son, who became King Charles I, was absolute. Increasingly, the king and the archbishop sought to rule the country without recourse to Parliament, and were if anything still more high-handed in Scotland, that resolutely Presbyterian nation that despised episcopacy. When, in 1637, James tried to impose on the Church of Scotland a version of the *Book of Common Prayer* that closely resembled the 1549 book in its embrace of traditionalism, riots broke out. The most famous tale of the conflict involves one Jenny Geddes, who, when a minister began saying the Communion service in Edinburgh's St. Giles Cathedral, threw a stool at the man and shouted, "Daur ye say Mass in my lug?" Presumably this story got around quickly, because when Bishop Whitford of Brechin read his first service from the prayer book he did so with two loaded pistols placed on the desk before him, in plain sight of the restive congregation.

Matters soon came to a climax in England as well. In late 1640, when Charles tried repeatedly to dismiss duly elected Parliaments whose views did not suit him, Parliament refused to be dismissed, and set about dismantling the work the king and his leading advisors had been doing for the past decade. They passed laws limiting royal power and arrested Archbishop Laud, along with the king's other primary advisor, Thomas Wentworth, Earl of Stratford, and imprisoned them in the Tower of London. (Stratford was executed in May 1641—the king, backed quite into a corner, even signed his death warrant—but Laud's political and legal position was more complex, and he shuttled between prison cell and court-room for years.) And a war against the prayer book was begun in earnest.

In December of 1640 a petition was submitted to Parliament with the signatures of thousands of Londoners, asking for radical changes in church government. It came to be known as the Root and Branch Petition because it requested that "the government of archbishops and lord bishops, deans, and archdeacons, &c., with their courts and ministrations in them . . . with all its dependencies, roots and branches, may be abolished, and all laws in their behalf made void, and the government according to God's word may be rightly placed amongst us." There followed the familiar protests against priests, altars, and the like, but these were coupled with stricter requirements. It was not sufficient, these petitioners and many thousands like them throughout England believed, to make minor adjustments to the existing *Book of Common Prayer*. Rather, "the Liturgy for the most part is framed out of the Romish breviary, rituals, mass-book, also the book of Ordination for archbishops and ministers framed out of the Roman Pontifical."[12] The whole book, in effect, would have to go, along with the ecclesiastical polity with which it had been hand in glove.

So it was that the need to control a king came to require also the radical restructuring of church government and banishment of the prayer book. About this linkage Cranmer and the evangelicals who ran the country under young King Edward could scarcely have complained; it was they, after all, who originally linked a particular form of common prayer with the government, employing the laws of the land to enforce its uniform use and strictly punish noncompliance. In the mid-seventeenth century Anglicans were forced to reap what their sixteenth-century predecessors had sown.

Rumors of the prayer book's forthcoming banishment agitated many whose lives—and, by this point, those of their parents and grandparents—had been formed by this book. In 1641, a group of Anglicans from Cheshire noted the increasing political dominance of Puritans like the Root and Branch petitioners. They made their own petition to Parliament, asking for the preservation of their beloved prayer book: Almost "any Family or Person that can read," they wrote, owns a copy of it, "in the conscionable Use whereof, many Christian Hearts have found unspeakable joy and Comfort; wherein the famous Church of England our dear Mother hath just Cause to Glory: and may she long flourish in the Practice of so blessed a liturgy." The *Book of Common Prayer* had in just a few generations become venerable, and among a wide range of English folk. It is customary, in light of later history and of certain famous novels, especially those of George Eliot, to think of Anglicans as the wealthy and powerful and Dissenters as the poor and marginalized, but this was not so clearly the case in the English Civil War era. Some of the leading opponents of episcopacy and the prayer book were of high social standing, and indeed could mock the lowliness of prayer-book defenders: one said that they were but "hedgers at the hedge, plowmen at the plow, threshers in the barns."[13]

But in any case the tide of events ran against those who loved the prayer book. More than a year before the abolition of episcopacy, and in the midst of a great civil war, Parliament banned its use. The prohibition became law on January 4, 1645—six days later Laud was beheaded on Tower Hill—and in August further laws were passed laying out the penalties for those caught using it. A century earlier, of course, punishment had awaited those who *failed* to use it, but the tables since had turned quite completely: the book mandated as the prayer book's replacement was the *Directory for the Public Worship of God*, commonly called the Public Directory, which was an adaptation of the order of worship John Knox developed in preference to the 1552 prayer book, whose papistry he had found so distasteful. The dogged and passionate Scot overcame Cranmer at last.

Meanwhile the war dragged on, Parliament against the king, in sufficiently inconsistent fashion that most historians refer to two civil wars: one lasting from 1642 to 1646, when Charles was taken prisoner and then passed from custodian to custodian; the second occurring in mid-1648, after Charles had negotiated a secret treaty with the Scots that called for them to invade England, which they failed successfully to do. Had Charles not made this treaty, he probably would have been restored to the throne with greatly reduced powers; instead, he was executed on January 4, 1649, four years to the day after the banishment of the *Book of Common Prayer*. Unlike Charles, the book survived.[14]

Once more we see a sixteenth-century pattern repeating itself: as the ascent of Queen Mary had sent many evangelicals fleeing to the Continent with their prayer books, so now a large body of Royalist Anglicans took *their* books with them to France, where they continued to pray according to the now-familiar rites, but in exile. As Horton Davies has pointed out, this proved to be a vital moment in the prayer book's history: during this period—variously called the Interregnum, the Commonwealth, or the Protectorate—"the Prayer Book had become the symbol of a secret, exciting, and prohibited worship (like the Mass for the English Recusants), and, even more significantly, the symbol of loyalty to a suffering church. Even in palmier days, it was never to lose this profound respect; as if it was necessary for it to have been prohibited for it to be fully appreciated."[15]

Those who remained in England employed various stratagems to continue, as best they could, their familiar forms of worship. They took full advantage of a certain vagueness to the Public Directory, which was not a prayer book as such, but a series of general guidelines for conducting worship that would ideally be characterized by a good deal of extemporaneous prayer. Robert Sanderson, who had been Regius Professor of Divinity at Oxford but found himself at the coming of the Commonwealth cast out into the wilds of Lincolnshire, where he tended the tiny parish of Boothby Pagnell, hoped that the obscurity of the place would allow him to conduct worship straight out of the *Book of Common Prayer*. But this was not to be. Some of Cromwell's soldiers observed him closely whenever he conducted services, and, according to his biographer, Isaak Walton, "would appear and visibly oppose him in the Church when he read the Prayers, some of them pretending to advise him how God was to be served more acceptably." Eventually, at the advice of a friend, Sanderson began to use the prayer book services, but with minor improvised deletions and additions, in order to create the impression that he was practicing the kind of freely extemporaneous service the Public Directory recommended. This worked well enough that he was never imprisoned or deprived of his parish.[16]

One of the most famous of the prayer-book exiles was John Evelyn, that remarkably curious man: diarist, antiquarian, founder of the Royal Society, arborphile, and the man responsible for introducing the tulip to England, setting off a decades-long craze. Several prayer books Evelyn and his family owned have survived, including a quarto edition from 1559—one of the very first of the Elizabethan prayer books—owned by his father-in-law, an English diplomat in France. When Evelyn and his wife took refuge there, they made a point of conducting daily prayers as a family according to the familiar rite. He found his world in Paris to be "a Little Britain and a kind of Sanctuary," even though some members of the French royal family were highly uncomfortable with non-Catholic services being performed under their noses and wanted to pronounce their own ban on prayer-book worship.[17]

Eventually Evelyn returned to England and resumed life at his estate, Sayes Court, on the south bank of the Thames in Kent. As the 1650s progressed he found it increasingly difficult to find public worship conducted according to the prayer book: the soldiers of the Commonwealth were growing increasingly vigilant. The observance of Christmas posed particular problems: for Evelyn and many of his fellow Anglicans it was one of the principal feasts of the church, but the Puritans forbade celebrating it, believing it to be superstitious papistry and painted-over paganism. In his diary for Christmas Day 1654, Evelyn writes, "No public offices in churches, but penalties to the observers, so I was constrain'd to celebrate it at home." But in London there were still services to be found; in his diary for 1657 he records, "I went with my Wife to London to celebrate *Christmas day,*" and after the sermon, as the congregation prepared to receive "the holy Sacrament, the chapel was surrounded with soldiers, and all the communicants and assembly surprised and kept by them, some in the house, others carried away." But before the soldiers took their prisoners, the people received Communion anyway. "These wretched miscreants, held their muskets against us as we came up to receive the Sacred Elements, as if they would have shot us at the Altar, yet suffering us to finish the office of Communion, as perhaps not having instructions what to do in case they found us in that action." All of Evelyn's language ("holy Sacrament," "Sacred Elements," and of course "Altar") testifies that he was a high churchman indeed, and one willing to take considerable risks to be known as such.[18]

But the exile of the prayer book was then drawing toward its end. Oliver Cromwell, the Lord Protector, died in September 1658, and many of the ablest revolutionary leaders had predeceased him. There being no obvious successor, his son, Richard, was put in his place, but Richard had few of his father's abilities, and, in this age of nearly universal monarchy, few even among the deposers of Charles I had confidence that a republican form of government could last. Negotiations commenced with Charles's son, who on his thirtieth birthday, May 29, 1660, entered London to general popular acclaim as the country's new king. Evelyn was there, and wrote in his diary,

> This day, his Majesty, Charles the Second came
> to London, after a sad and long exile and calami-
> tous suffering both of the King and Church,

being seventeen years. This was also his birthday, and with a triumph of above 20,000 horse
and foot, brandishing their swords, and shout-
ing with inexpressible joy; the ways strewed
with flowers, the bells ringing, the streets hung
with tapestry, fountains running with wine; the
Mayor, Aldermen, and all the Companies, in
their liveries, chains of gold, and banners; Lords
and Nobles, clad in cloth of silver, gold, and
velvet; the windows and balconies, all set with
ladies; trumpets, music, and myriads of people
flocking, even so far as from Rochester, so as they
were seven hours in passing the city, even from
two in the afternoon till nine at night.

I stood in the Strand and beheld it, and
blessed God.[19]

And just as the fall of the monarchy had required
the fall of episcopacy and the prayer book, so too the
Restoration restored those forces. Once again there
would be a Church of England whose worship was
governed by a *Book of Common Prayer*. The question
was: What would this book contain?

Some English churchmen had been meditating
on this question for quite some time. The two most
important of them had very different experiences
during the Interregnum: one led an active, energetic
life in Paris, while the other passed his time imprisoned in the Tower of London. The prisoner was
the Bishop of Ely, Matthew Wren, a former Master

of Peterhouse, Cambridge, and a close associate of Archbishop Laud. (Christopher Wren, greatest of English architects, was his nephew.) The other key figure, John Cosin, succeeded Wren as Master of Peterhouse, where he demonstrated his own Laudian principles by having a lavish chapel built in a more-or-less Gothic style, thus anticipating the Gothic Revival by two hundred years. When Cosin was expelled from Peterhouse and fled to the Continent, Puritans, for whom its statues and decorations were pure papistry, destroyed much of the interior of the chapel. In fact, Cosin, for all his high-church preferences, was quite hostile to Catholicism, and in Paris befriended the local Huguenots and worked hard to prevent his fellow Anglicans from "crossing the Tiber." He also served as a chaplain to aristocrats and members of the royal family in exile.

Despite his many and varied responsibilities, Cosin found time during his seventeen years in Paris to study the prayer book carefully and make extended notes on it, with the hope that someday, when king and episcopacy were restored, there might be the opportunity to issue a new and improved edition. Wren's lonelier thoughts moved along the same path. So when the monarchy was restored, and Cosin and Wren were likewise restored to their former places, they found themselves with the chance to implement the revisions they had so long contemplated. But getting the various concerned parties to agree on what the book should say proved no easier now than it had in the sixteenth century. Cosin and Wren wanted to shift it toward their own high-church sensibilities, and therefore were partial to the 1549 book, coupled with some insistently Laudian rubrics; Anglicans of a more Reformed persuasion, like the brilliant and charitable but stubborn Richard Baxter, played a role similar to the one John Knox had played in relation to Cranmer; and a third group, insistent on returning in every respect to the *status quo ante bellum*, wanted precisely the book their mothers and fathers had used: the Elizabethan book from 1559 with the minor revisions that had been introduced in 1604. It took two years to sort these matters out.

Much of the sorting out was done in the Savoy Conference, which met in 1661 between April and July and featured debates between traditionalist Anglicans like Wren and Cosin on one side and, on the other, mostly Presbyterians—Presbyterians being the Puritan party most amenable to Anglican practices, though, as it turned out, not amenable enough to make the conference run smoothly. (Those who dissented most strongly from the Anglican church-state model, Congregationalists and Baptists and Quakers and Diggers and Ranters, were not invited to the conference and probably would not have come anyway.) The strongest minds and wills on both sides were also the most politically naive; it is hard to imagine that Cosin truly believed that it would be possible to reinstate the communion rails that Laud had used to enforce his policy of kneeling during Communion, to the bonfire-making resentment of so many, yet he insisted on just that. Similarly, on the Presbyterian side, the fluent and prolific Baxter arrived at the conference, saw that the high-church party wanted to know precisely what the Presbyterians preferred, and wrote an entire prayer book, later known as the Savoy Liturgy, in two weeks. He then cheerfully presented this to the whole conference in the apparent expectation that it would be deemed acceptable.[20]

In the end, the conference was inconclusive, though the high-church party did agree to the Presbyterian demand that Scripture readings in the new book be taken from the Authorized Version. (But they retained Coverdale's version of the Psalms, as it had become woven into their hearts through the prominence of the Psalms in all Cranmer's rites.) The *Book of Common Prayer* that eventually emerged followed neither Cosin's model nor Baxter's, though it did end up incorporating many of Cosin and Wren's revisions. Cosin owned a 1619 edition of the prayer book in which he had written meticulous and extensive notes on passages that he thought ought to be altered, either because he wanted to return to the more traditionalist liturgy of 1549, or because he wanted the rubrics to be clearer and more specific, or because he thought that certain terms had become outdated. To this book he added similar suggestions from Wren, and this—because Cosin was now the Prince-Bishop of Durham—became known as the Durham Book.[21] When serious work on a revised prayer book began in November of 1661 by the Convocation of Canterbury—the whole assembly of English clergy, comprised of an Upper House of Bishops and a Lower House of Priests, under the general governance of the Archbishop of Canterbury, Gilbert Sheldon—the Durham Book was used to help make necessary corrections, but none of the substantive changes that Cosin or Wren had recommended were accepted. That the alterations to the 1604 book were minor may be testified to by this one signal fact: the Convocation did its work of producing a new prayer book in twenty-two days. They wrapped up their work on December 18; the king gave his assent on May 19, 1662; and the book was deemed the law of the land by a new Act of Uniformity, to take effect on St. Bartholomew's Day, August 24. It has been the official *Book of Common Prayer* of the Church of England ever since, though, as will become clear, that status does not mean nearly as much now as it did in 1662.

The preface to the book was largely written by Robert Sanderson, whom we last saw being heckled by Puritan soldiers in Boothby Pagnell, but who now had risen to be Bishop of Lincoln and worked closely with Wren and Cosin to get the new book properly edited. In the preface he is most concerned to insist that Convocation made changes only when they were deemed absolutely necessary. After all, there was, strictly speaking, nothing *wrong* with the old book: "We are fully persuaded in our judgements (and we here profess it to the world) that the Book, as it stood before established by Law, doth not contain in it any thing contrary to the Word of God, or to sound Doctrine, or which a godly man may not with a good Conscience use and submit unto." With this in mind, the preface goes on to say that three general kinds of changes had been made. First came those "for the better direction of them that are to officiate in any part of Divine Service," which meant primarily clarification of the instructional rubrics. The second group of changes was "for the more proper expressing of some words or phrases of ancient usage in terms more suitable to the language of the present times, and the clearer explanation of some other words and phrases, that were either of doubtful signification, or otherwise liable to misconstruction." Here was some attempt to pacify Puritans who feared that a popish construction could be placed on some terms, though not all these changes made Puritans happy: most grievously, the officiant at Communion is termed "Priest" rather than "Minister." The third category involved "a more perfect rendering of such portions of holy Scripture, as are inserted into the Liturgy," that is to say, replacement of the sixteenth-century translation with the Authorized Version.

The preface further notes that a few prayers for particular occasions, and for the monarchy itself, had been added. Charles I was recognized as a martyr. Among the more striking new prayers in the 1662 book are the "Forms of Prayer to be Used at Sea," an indication of England's ever-increasing sense of itself as a maritime power around the world. These include prayers "to be also used in her Majesty's Navy every day"—one of which begins, "O eternal Lord God, who alone spreadest out the heavens, and rulest the raging of the sea"—and prayers for particular circumstances, including one for success in naval battle and two for salvation from storms: "Look down, we beseech thee, and hear us, calling out of the depth of misery, and out of the jaws of this death, which is ready now to swallow us up: Save, Lord, or else we perish." These are accompanied by brief, one-sentence prayers to be used in occasions of great urgency, when the crew cannot gather to pray corporately, and psalms appointed for "Thanksgiving after a Storm." To read these prayers is to be immersed in a drama, almost as happens to the reader of Patrick O'Brian's novels about the Royal Navy during the Napoleonic Wars—novels in which we hear these prayers said many times, with fervor corresponding to the demands of the moment, or lack thereof.

The first sentence of the preface is perhaps the signal statement of the familiar idea that the Church of England seeks a via media, a middle way, between Roman Catholicism and reformed Protestantism—but here that way is cast in terms of flexibility of order: "It hath been the wisdom of the Church of England, ever since the first compiling of her Public

Liturgy, to keep the mean between the two extremes, of too much stiffness in refusing, and of too much easiness in admitting any variation from it."[22] Cosin, in his Laudian way, had wanted nearly everything prescribed that could be prescribed; the Presbyterians by contrast pleaded for more freedom, though not as much as those (like Milton) who disdained all set forms. Indeed, the Presbyterians believed that *they* embodied the via media: as they wrote during the Savoy Conference, "We would avoid both the extreme that would have no form, and the contrary extreme that would have nothing but forms." They desired to have room to *punctuate* the set prayers with extemporaneous ones: for them the celebrated concision of Cranmer's formulations could at times be a spiritual straitjacket. On this point they are eloquent:

> Prayer and humility are, indeed, the necessary means of peace; but if you will let us pray for peace in no words but are in the Common Prayer book, their brevity and unaptness, and the customariness, that will take off the edge of fervor with human nature, will not give leave (or help sufficient) to our souls to work towards God, upon this subject, with that enlargedness, copiousness, and freedom as is necessary to true fervor. A brief, transient touch and away, is not enough to warm the heart aright; and cold prayers are likely to have a cold return.

But that eloquence did not win the day, any more than did Cosin's beloved Communion rails. The makers of the revision knew their decisions would displease many parties, but Sanderson concludes the preface with the hope that it would be "well accepted and approved by all sober, peaceable, and truly conscientious Sons of the Church of *England*." That hope would not be realized, though the prayer book would find success in ways, and in places, that Sanderson and his coworkers could not have imagined.

FIGURE 4. Beginning soon after its first publication in 1549, the *Book of Common Prayer* was translated into many other languages. This rare late seventeenth-century copy renders the book in shorthand.

By permission of the Folger Shakespeare Library.

The Book in the Social World

CHAPTER 4

An unintended consequence of the Restoration was the creation of Dissent, or Nonconformity, as a permanent category, a fixed point on the religious landscape of Britain. Of course, there had always been people who rejected the Church of England, from Roman Catholics to Quakers and Diggers, but at the Restoration their legal situation came to a point of crisis. It proved, though, to be a wavering sort of point. Charles II, at least at the outset of his reign, showed a good deal of forbearance toward the Dissenters, whom he knew to be still a powerful interest in English society, and he seems always to have been sympathetic to Roman Catholicism, even long before he was received into that church on his deathbed. But Gilbert Sheldon, the Archbishop of Canterbury, did not share Charles's breadth of tolerance. Deeply Laudian in his commitments, he felt that he had already admitted massive concessions into the new *Book of Common Prayer* and thought it appropriate to insist on strict and detailed fidelity to the new book, and to the episcopal system of governance that underlay it. No one would be granted the right to be called, and to practice as, a Christian minister who had not been ordained by a bishop of the Church of England, and those who were so ordained would be monitored closely for compliance with the theology, the liturgies, and the rubrics of the prayer book. This new Act of Uniformity came into law on the same day the new book was approved, which meant that most of those required to swear loyalty to that book had not yet seen it and were not sure what it would say.

As time went on, conformity to the *Book of Common Prayer* would be understood primarily in terms of the Articles of Religion, or the Thirty-Nine Articles as they were familiarly called. These articles— which are not intrinsic to the prayer book as such, but are usually included in editions of it—had their origin in attempts during the reign of Henry VIII to state precisely what this new English church believed once it ceased to take its theological direction from Rome. First came the Ten Articles of 1536, followed by the Six Articles three years later, and then in Edward's reign the Forty-Two Articles. In 1563 the articles were determined to be neither more nor fewer than thirty-nine, and at that number they would remain. But only with the Restoration did submission to the articles become a kind of shorthand for submission to the authority of the Church of England as a whole, and for many laypersons as well as the church's clergy. In 1673 and 1678 the two Test Acts were passed, requiring anyone who wished to hold civil office in England to subscribe to the articles. Prospective students at Oxford and Cambridge had to affirm them to be admitted and to affirm them again to receive a degree. These expectations for politicians, civil servants, and students would be repealed in the nineteenth century, but as long as they lasted they led to some extraordinary intellectual gymnastics, as ambitious young men strove to convince figures of authority (and sometimes themselves) that they warmly endorsed doctrines they in fact cared nothing for or actively despised.

When the Act of Uniformity was passed in 1662, approximately two thousand ministers of the Church of England, most of them Puritans and none of them inclined to intellectual agility, refused to swear the oath of loyalty and were summarily defrocked in what came to be known as the Great Ejection. For some years the government, driven largely by the archbishop, tried to enforce a very hard line in these matters: in 1664 it passed the Conventicle Act to prohibit groups of more than five people from meeting to worship; a year later came the Five Mile Act, which forbade those who had been ejected from coming within five miles of their former parishes or indeed any incorporated town, and likewise forbade them from working as teachers. But it was palpably impossible to enforce such draconian laws with any consistency, as the Puritans themselves had learned when trying to prohibit prayer-book worship, and long before an Act of Toleration was passed in 1689, the first year of the reign of William and Mary, it had become clear that the established church was just one option among several for the Christian believer. Bishop Sanderson's image of "all sober, peaceable, and truly conscientious Sons of the Church of *England*" being unified by their commitment to the *Book of Common Prayer* dissolved into thin air. The prayer book would never again provide the central and governing rites of the nation. Most English men and women would hear its cadences only at the weightiest moments of life—baptism, marriage, burial—and many would never hear them at all.

In the 150 years following the Restoration the English people were not especially religious in any form. Recent research suggests that the Church of England itself was not quite as thoroughly moribund in the eighteenth century as it was long thought to have been, but there were certainly evident forms of decline: as Roy Porter has noted, in 1714 seventy-two churches in London offered daily services, but only fourteen years later that number had declined to fifty-two; by 1732 only forty-four churches in London offered Morning Prayer daily. Further, "in mid-century Oxfordshire, only about one person took communion for every three families. . . . Thirty Oxford parishes which between them had 911 communicants in 1738 had just 685 in 1802. Only about one in ten English people took Easter Communion with the national church in 1801."[1] Cranmer had hoped for an England in which the great majority of the people went to church to pray twice each day, with a Communion service added after Morning Prayer each Sunday; 90 percent of English folk neglecting to take Communion on Easter would have struck him as national apostasy. And this neglect was caused, at least in part, by indifference and incompetence on the part of the church, which allowed many areas to go underserved by priests, or scarcely served at all. Porter again:

> The London Churches Act of 1711 set money aside to erect churches, but only ten out of a projected fifty were actually constructed, largely because the trustees opted for a small number of architectural gems rather than the full quota of functional ones. Manchester, whose population by the late eighteenth century exceeded 20,000 people, had but one parish church, as did the Marylebone section of London, with a population of twice that of Manchester. (St. Marylebone Church, built only in 1740 to replace a dilapidated medieval structure, seated just 200.)

Porter understates when he writes, "The year 1800 dawned with the Anglican Church ill-equipped to serve the nation."[2]

So the image of one nation bound together by one use and one book, sometimes put forth by lovers of the prayer book, is a consoling fiction. But it is an understandable fiction: the *Book of Common Prayer* would for the next two centuries and more have a disproportionate influence among the social and cultural elite, who would hear it read and make their responses in church—when they came to church—but also in their homes, at their schools and universities, at the Inns of Court. Thanks to the conservatism of these institutions, their relationship to the prayer book changed very little until well into the twentieth century. And given their role in establishing social norms, the prayer book's social and cultural influence would be far greater than the number of its strict adherents would suggest.

The prayer-book exiles during the Commonwealth—whether their exile was literal or internal—developed the habit of saying their daily prayers at home. We saw that John Evelyn had recourse to this practice only reluctantly, but for many families it may have been preferable. It appears that, among the gentry at least, the head of the family saw leading family prayers from the prayer book as intrinsic to his duties, though of course, some took these duties more seriously than did others. In Thackeray's *Vanity Fair* (1847), we see that Mr. Osborne is reminded of his spiritual duties only on "those rare Sunday evenings when there was no dinner-party, and when the great scarlet Bible and Prayer-book were taken out from the corner where they stood beside his copy of the Peerage, and the servants being rung up to the dining parlour"; at such times "Osborne read the evening service to his family in a loud grating pompous voice." Somewhat later in the novel we see the different, and somewhat more disciplined, practice of Sir Pitt Crawley, who added the reading of a sermon to the performance of Morning Prayer: "A book of family sermons, one of which Sir Pitt was in the habit of administering to his family on Sunday mornings, lay ready on the study table, and awaiting his judicious selection." These "family sermons" were written by divines precisely for such home gatherings, though it's doubtful that the divines would have been happy with a gentleman who read out their sermons *instead of* taking his family to church, which seems to have been Sir Pitt's practice. At least his spiritual leadership was habitual, rather than merely occasional.[3] However, Sir Pitt evidently lacked the rigor of a seventeenth-century Cheshire gentleman, John Bruen, who began each day by ringing a bell through his house to summon everyone to their prayers, in imitation of the familiar bell ringing of the parish church.[4]

The very wealthy could demonstrate their commitment to family prayers—and avoid having to go to church at all—by building chapels for their country houses and hiring (often impoverished) priests to serve as their domestic chaplains. In Jane Austen's *Mansfield Park*, when Maria Bertram plans to marry a rich but otherwise undistinguished man named Rushworth, Rushworth's widowed mother gives the Bertram clan a tour of her country house. As they visit the chapel she comments, "It is a handsome chapel, and was formerly in constant use both morning and evening. Prayers were always read in it by the domestic chaplain, within the memory of many; but the late Mr. Rushworth left it off." To this news the superficial but witty Mary Crawford remarks, "Every generation has its improvements"—which in turn elicits a surprisingly sharp outburst from Austen's painfully shy heroine, Maria's cousin Fanny Price:

> "It is a pity," cried Fanny, "that the custom should have been discontinued. It was a valuable part of former times. There is something in a chapel and chaplain so much in character with a great house, with one's ideas of what such a household should be! A whole family assembling regularly for the purpose of prayer is fine!"

Although there can be little doubt where Austen's sympathies lie, she allows Mary Crawford to defend her position with some vigor: Mary is surely right to point out that this practice had to be tiring for the household servants, who had enough to do already.

Whether or not Mary's compassion for the Rushworth servants is genuine, and whether or not one agrees with her admiration for the lapsing of that family's commitment to daily prayer, the scene is a useful reminder that the English aristocracy and gentry were taught to be responsible for the spiritual nurture of those who worked for them; we see this also in the Osborne family, whose servants were "rung up to the dining parlour" when the head of the family decided that it was time for Evening Prayer and a sermon. Among the English people who knew the prayer book best would have been the often-illiterate servants of the rich.

The children of the family were present for such prayers as well, so when the boys went off to school—as some of them did as early as age eight—they heard their headmasters read the same services they knew from home. How many of them were conscious and alert enough to notice this cannot be said; among the many complaints Englishmen have uttered over the centuries about their schooldays, those concerning catatonia-inducing chapel services may come in second only to those concerning food. In one of his essays George Orwell remembers the gratitude he and his fellow students felt for an assistant master who, when given charge of Morning Prayer in the absence of the headmaster, would ignore the lectionary and read to them from the more colorful sections of the Apocrypha.[5]

This association of prayer book worship with sheer coercion would continue for those who went up to Cambridge or Oxford, at least until the universities waived the requirement to affirm the Articles of Religion and started accepting non-Anglican, and indeed non-Christian, students in the mid-nineteenth century. This broadening of undergraduate religion posed quite a problem for the custom of compulsory chapel attendance—How could you force non-Anglicans to attend Morning Prayer each day?—but the collegiate authorities were reluctant to abandon a requirement they themselves had suffered under. Their solution was devilish: students were required to attend chapel or to inform the chaplain that they would not be attending, but if they opted for the latter had to buttonhole the chaplain *before* the service began. So one could escape chapel only by getting up earlier than chapelgoers. This kept the chapels reasonably full until the cruelty of the practice became too obvious and compulsion was abandoned altogether. C. S. Lewis would later comment on the widespread belief that the empty chapels of Oxford and Cambridge marked a "decline of religion" in the universities. "Now it is quite true," he wrote, "that chapels which were quite full in 1900 are empty in 1946. But this change was not gradual. It occurred at the precise moment when chapel ceased to be compulsory. It was not in fact a decline; it was a precipice. . . . The withdrawal of compulsion did not create a new religious situation, but only revealed the situation which had long existed."[6]

In any event, bodily presence did not mean spiritual conformity, and in the universities, as in the public schools, people found ways to announce their rebellion: Cyril Connolly, at Balliol in the 1920s, refused to bow his head during the Creed, and while others sang the hymns he perused a volume of Petronius: "I had four editions of the *Satyricon*. The best I had bound in black crushed levant and kept on my pew in chapel where it looked like some solemn book of devotion and was never disturbed."[7]

The prayer book was, then, associated in the minds of many people with various forms of compulsion: it was among the more common things that your teachers made you do, or your parents, or (if you were a servant) your masters. Civic duty also required that you bow to it, for it represented, and with it you prayed for, your monarch and your country. Visitors to England assumed this was generally an acceptable state of affairs: thus George Santayana's comment that "the Englishman finds that he was born a Christian, and therefore wishes to remain a Christian; but . . . it is an axiom with him that nothing can be obligatory for a Christian which is unpalatable to an Englishman."[8] But it was often the case that people came to appreciate the beauty and the power of the prayer book only when they achieved some removal from the coercive mechanisms with which it was entangled. Old Boys of the various public schools, and graduates of the old universities, often recalled chapel and the accompanying sonorities of the prayer book with nostalgic fondness, as they also recalled being flogged for being caught out in their Latin declensions.

Moreover, rebellion is always relative to the authority from which one rebels. The philosopher Roger Scruton grew up in an unbelieving home, but his father "wished his children to graduate to atheism from a heritage of Nonconformist gloom" and learn to hate everything Anglican, since the Church of England was for him "one arm of the ruling conspiracy that cast a shadow over England." So he sent his children to the local chapels, first Methodist and then Baptist. But fifteen-year-old Roger fell in love with Anglican architecture and the liturgy of the *Book of Common Prayer*. "My father believed that I went each Sunday morning to the Baptist chapel, having inexplicably rediscovered a desire to inspect my sins. I excused the lie, since it was told on God's behalf." The young man liked the local parish's high-church vicar, whose "services were conducted to the letter of the Book of Common Prayer, and his sermons were elaborations of its poetry."[9]

📖

It is almost universal to praise the *Book of Common Prayer* for the beauty of its language, and has been for a long time. Even by the beginning of the eighteenth century it had taken on a kind of archaic stateliness. Jonathan Swift, writing in 1712, comments that the Authorized Version of the Bible and the prayer book, "those Books being perpetually read in Churches, have proved a kind of Standard for Language, especially to the common People. And I doubt whether the Alterations since introduced, have added much to the Beauty or Strength of the English Tongue, though they have taken off a great deal from that Simplicity, which is one of the greatest Perfections in any Language." This commendation comes from

Swift's "Proposal for Correcting, Improving, and Ascertaining the English Tongue," where he argues that deep acquaintance with those books provides a foundation for a good English style.[10]

And many, in their private moments, found in the prayer book language not just stately but also capable of expressing their deepest spiritual needs and longings. Samuel Johnson, who as a deeply patriotic man was untroubled by the prayer book's association with civic authority, also found that the book's language, especially that of Cranmer's collects, gave shape and form to his own spiritual turmoil. The urgency of Cranmer's petitions was perhaps felt more strongly in his own day than it would be later—archaic language rarely seems as emotionally wrought as contemporary usage does—but Johnson certainly felt it. It seems that Johnson received Communion rarely, but always on Easter, and took the conclusion of Holy Week, Good Friday through Easter day, as an opportunity for self-examination. He did not like what he saw, and in attempts to master his agonies of remorse composed his own Cranmer-like collects. On Easter eve 1761 he wrote,

> Almighty and most merciful Father, look down upon my misery with pity, strengthen me that I may overcome all sinful habits, grant that I may with effectual faith commemorate the death of thy Son Jesus Christ, so that all corrupt desires may be extinguished, and all vain thoughts may

be dispelled. Enlighten me with true knowledge, animate me with reasonable hope, comfort me with a just sense of thy love, and assist me to the performance of all holy purposes, that after the sins, errors, and miseries of this world, I may obtain everlasting happiness for Jesus Christ's sake. To whom, &c. Amen.[11]

This is more elaborate that Cranmer would have made it, but Johnson was adapting a Cranmerian form for his own purposes, and the styles of the two men rhyme closely. Similarly, on "Sept. 18, 1768, at night," he writes, "I have now begun the sixtieth year of my life. How the last year has passed I am unwilling to terrify myself with thinking." Johnson suffered from deep depressions, or what he called "the black dog," and the silence and solitude of the night were dreadful to him, especially after the death of his wife. It is therefore telling that he continues by writing, "O Lord, who hast safely brought me, &c."—an invocation of the Collect for Grace from Morning, not Evening, Prayer:

O Lord, our heavenly Father, Almighty and everlasting God, who hast safely brought us to the beginning of this day; Defend us in the same with thy mighty power; and grant that this day we fall into no sin, neither run into any kind of danger; but that all our doings may be ordered by thy governance, to do always that is righteous in thy sight; through Jesus Christ our Lord. Amen.

Johnson clearly felt himself in need of God's defending, but his echo also suggests that his anxieties had kept him up late into the night and perhaps into the morning. He would have known that in the old *horae canonicae* Matins was said at three a.m. and ended near dawn; he would also have felt, in his own way, the rightness of the old prayers' acknowledgment of the fears of the night and relief at surviving them. His personal collects often seek deliverance from fear:

> Deliver and preserve me from vain terrors . . .
> Heal my body, strengthen my mind, compose my distraction, calm my inquietude, and relieve my terrors . . .
> Have mercy upon me, O God, have mercy upon me; years and infirmities oppress me, terror and anxiety beset me. Have mercy upon me, my Creator and my Judge. In all dangers protect me, in all perplexities relieve and free me, and so help me by thy Holy Spirit, that I may now so commemorate the death of thy Son our Savior Jesus Christ as that when this short and painful life shall have an end, I may for his sake be received to everlasting happiness. Amen.

The sonorous cadences, the elegant repetitions and antitheses, of Cranmer's prose may strike some as cold; we recall the Puritans' complaints at the Savoy Conference: "A brief, transient touch and away, is not enough to warm the heart aright." Johnson, however, did not need his heart warmed, but rather his racing mind calmed. For him, and for many who have felt themselves at the mercy of chaotic forces from within or without, the style of the prayer book has healing powers. It provides equitable balance when we ourselves have none.

📖

As one of the greatest masters of English prose, Johnson would have been unusually attuned to the prayer book's cadences, but others needed some help. They could get that help from a minister who read the services properly. In Austen's *Mansfield Park*, there is a lively conversation on this topic between Edmund Bertram, who is about to take holy orders, and Henry Crawford: "Crawford proceeded to ask [Edmund's] opinion and give his own as to the properest manner in which particular passages in the service should be delivered, shewing it to be a subject on which he had thought before, and thought with judgment." But Crawford's thoughts are not wholly connected with piety: when we read his reflections we must remember that he is a young man with a particular interest in and gift for acting.

> "Our liturgy," observed Crawford, "has beauties, which not even a careless, slovenly style of reading can destroy; but it has also redundancies and repetitions which require good reading not to be

felt. For myself, at least, I must confess being not always so attentive as I ought to be . . . nineteen times out of twenty I am thinking how such a prayer ought to be read, and longing to have it to read myself."

Crawford goes on to speak of preaching as another mode of rhetorical performance in which he would like to excel, as long as he did not have to do it very often.

This is meant to show Crawford's frivolous inconstancy, but even the pious were rarely indifferent to such matters. The greatest English preacher of the eighteenth century, George Whitefield, went up to Oxford hoping to become an actor; his conversion and subsequent career change did not end his interest in oratorical excellence but rather redirected it. It was common throughout the reign of the prayer book for people to assess their minister's commitment to Christian truth not just by his sermons but also by the clarity and emphasis with which he read the offices; such readings could be reprobated either for rushed mumbling or for pompous orotundity.

These judgments could be more easily made in the kinds of churches that came into fashion soon after the Restoration: these "auditory churches"—as Christopher Wren, the greatest of their architects, called them—are open, airy, well-lit spaces, often circular in shape, where services can be easily heard, and likewise seen in one's own prayer book. They are something like the opposite of Gothic churches, those darkened divided chambers designed to enfold the holy mysteries of the Mass. The auditory churches fit a religion almost wholly of the book: they are made not for Holy Communion but for Morning Prayer and Evensong, complete with learned or perhaps just hortatory sermons. They were meant for congregational participation as well: clearly audible in them are not just the minister's prayers but also the people's responses. Had Cranmer lived to hear the words he wrote celebrated in such spaces, about that, at least, he would have been delighted—as long as the priest made sure to say the prayers "in a loud voice."

📖

The major religious event of the eighteenth century in England, and in North America as well, was the rise of modern evangelicalism. Two Anglicans dominated this development: George Whitefield and John Wesley. But though Whitefield came to serious Christian faith largely through his association with John and Charles Wesley, and they later worked together for a time in a shared evangelistic enterprise, they represented different strains of Anglicanism, and quite different approaches to the *Book of Common Prayer*. Their chief theological disagreement was over the doctrine of predestination, which the Calvinist Whitefield not only believed but thought to be essential to the Gospel he preached, but which

Wesley considered to be a deeply pernicious doctrine. Through several decades they debated this matter, sometimes in person, sometimes via letter, but most commonly through dueling publications. But more telling for our purposes here are their very differing views on the nature of worship and the value of set forms.

Whitefield cared nothing for them. Although a priest in the Church of England, and therefore bound when leading services in its parishes to use the prayer book and follow its rubrics, he was largely unaffected by these strictures because he pursued the career of an itinerant preacher. When allowed to preach in churches he did so, but he was rarely invited to do so. For one thing, many Anglican ministers disliked the open and extravagant emotionalism of his preaching. One friend commented, "I hardly ever knew him to go through a sermon without weeping . . . sometimes he exceedingly wept, stamped loudly and passionately, and was frequently so overcome, that, for a few seconds, you would suspect he never could recover."[12] But recover he would, and often near the end of the sermon grabbed a black cap of the kind that judges wore when giving sentence, placed it on his head, and pronounced a verdict of death to sinners. Whitefield was a virtuoso of homiletic histrionics and drew audiences so large that they could not crowd their way into most churches, which was another reason he rarely got invited to preach. It was better for all concerned if he just preached outdoors, which he did for most of his career. Indeed, he died in Newburyport, Massachusetts, just hours after preaching a two-hour open-air sermon.

For such a preacher, focused so absolutely on bringing the Good News of Jesus Christ to lost souls, and especially to the illiterate poor, the *Book of Common Prayer* seemed less than relevant. But for John Wesley, who was a serious churchman all his life and focused not just on saving the lost—though he preached many evangelistic sermons too—but on helping Christians to grow in holiness, the prayer book was essential. "I believe there is no liturgy in the world," he wrote, "either in ancient or modern language, which breathes more a solid, scriptural, rational piety, than the Common Prayer of the Church of England."[13] Even late in his life, when his Methodists had come to be seen as rivals to the established church, he said of himself that he was a "High Churchman, the son of a High Churchman, bred up from my childhood in the highest notions of passive obedience and non-resistance" to the reigning authorities.[14] Thus by calling the prayer book "rational" Wesley meant to give it high praise: it is sensible, orderly, well-organized—just the sort of document to help people form the regular disciplines needed to be faithful Christians. (It should always be remembered that before becoming the leader of a large religious movement Wesley was an Oxford tutor.) Yet Wesley, though his own preaching was mild and quiet in comparison to the scenery-chewing Whitefield, believed in the need for powerful emotional experiences, particular moments in life when God gave the grace to live perfectly—which in Wesley's vocabulary meant without conscious, intentional sin—and exhorted his listeners and followers to seek them out and treasure them. So when more sober and plodding Christians called Wesley a promoter of religious enthusiasm, they were essentially correct.

Moreover, as Methodism developed Wesley came to promote the creation of a revised prayer book for Methodists' use, though all the time insisting he was a faithful son of the Church of England. The rise of modern evangelicalism, whether in its focus on Whitefield-style preaching or Wesleyan cultivation of deep and lasting holiness, had a strong tendency to push the *Book of Common Prayer* into the background of the Christian life. At the other end of the religious spectrum, for the Latitudinarians, with their focus on true religion as the keeping of a few not-especially-demanding moral guidelines, Cranmer's elegant liturgical formulations were largely irrelevant. As the eighteenth century wore on, it seemed that, while few except for old Dissenters sought to eliminate the prayer book entirely, most English men and women had little care for it. If for the seventeenth-century prayer-book exiles like John Evelyn the book had become venerable, a century later it might be better described as musty. But the next century would show that there was a good deal of life in the old book yet.

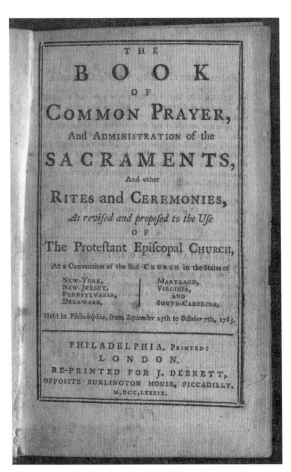

FIGURE 5. The first *Book of Common Prayer* for the new Protestant Episcopal Church of the United States (1789). Note that this edition is reprinted in London from the first Philadelphia printing.

Photograph courtesy of the Francis Donaldson Library at Nashotah House Theological Seminary.

Objects, Bodies, and Controversies

CHAPTER 5

Many stories, few of which are demonstrably true, describe the adventures of that great Elizabethan Sir Francis Drake. One that has been told since Elizabeth still sat on the throne goes like this: Throughout the first half of 1579, Drake's ship the *Golden Hind* pirated and plundered its way up the Pacific coast of South America. Killing and stealing from Spaniards was hard and dangerous work, so by the time the *Hind* reached California the ship and its crew were rather battered. On June 21, the crew found a safe and quiet harbor where they could anchor the ship, perform some essential repairs, and take on water and such supplies as were available. Some historians think this harbor was San Francisco Bay, though more of them prefer the significantly named Drake's Bay, some thirty miles north. But wherever the ship landed, it landed on a Sunday, and the crew came ashore so that the chaplain, Francis Fletcher, could lead them in the service of Morning Prayer. And so a service from the *Book of Common Prayer* was read in America for the first time.[1]

The first service of Holy Communion from the prayer book, as far as we know, was conducted in May of 1607, in the new colony of Jamestown in Virginia. But the book was already, by then, entangled in the English colonial enterprise in a variety of ways. The first Welsh version of the *Book of Common Prayer*—*Y Llyfr Gweddi Gyffredin*—was published in 1567, in obedience to a parliamentary order; the first Irish translation appeared in 1606, and the first Manx one in 1610. Eventually translations of the prayer book appeared in every part of the world where the British Empire cast its shadow and a few places where it never did; for instance, before the 1549 prayer book was even finished, its order for Holy Communion appeared in German, most likely translated by Andreas Osiander, the uncle of Cranmer's wife. But in the American colonies it had an especially interesting and politically fraught history.

That history varied dramatically according to the latitude of a given colony. In the South, where many Anglicans lived but where churches were few and far between, a strong culture developed of household services from the prayer book.[2] But in New England, where so many of the settlers had crossed the sea to escape the demands of the Anglican system, the prayer book was at best a symbol of oppression and at worst a tool of the Romish Satan. When Samuel Johnson— not the Great Cham of Literature cited in the previous chapter, but an eighteenth-century Congregationalist minister from Connecticut—was persuaded by the beauty and incisiveness of the prayer book that Anglicanism was right and godly, and thereupon sailed to England to receive properly apostolic ordination, he created outrage all over New England. When he returned in 1724 to start a new church, it was the first Anglican church in all of Connecticut.

Thirty years later Johnson answered the call of the vestrymen of Trinity Church in New York City (now known as Trinity Wall Street) to head up a new college, which they planned to call King's College in keeping with the royalism of most American Anglicans. In the few years he served as the new institution's first president, he strove to make it as explicitly Anglican as possible, and to build his students' spiritual lives around the disciplines of the prayer book. During the Revolutionary War classes were suspended—though not before King's had educated such students as Alexander Hamilton, John Jay, and Gouverneur Morris—and when the institution reopened in 1784, in a newly independent country, its old name no longer seemed quite so appropriate. It was rechristened Columbia College, later Columbia University.

The same discomfort that prompted King's College to change its name had other consequences as well; in fact, it led to one of the most signal events in the history of the *Book of Common Prayer*. Thanks to the American Revolution, it became evident to all that the prayer book had ceased to be one book; it became, for the first time, as much a historical document as a manual of devotion. However, this historicizing process did not begin with the American Revolution; the achievement of the colonies' independence simply gave new impetus to a movement that could be said to have begun in Edinburgh, when Jenny Geddes threw her stool at the bishop.

Perhaps no one fully understands the enormous complexities of the history of Scottish Anglicanism; certainly even the main threads cannot be untangled here. But a few points can be made clear. The service Jenny Geddes protested so memorably was called Laud's Liturgy, though Archbishop Laud did not write it and many scholars believe he did not even strongly endorse it: he probably would have preferred using the same prayer book throughout the two kingdoms. Its forcible rejection was soon followed by the upheavals of the English Civil War, and even some decades later the ecclesiastical-political situation in Scotland remained chaotic; when Charles II came to the throne in 1660, episcopacy was technically restored to Scotland, but in practice the old Scottish preference for a presbyterian system of church governance remained in place. After the deposition of James II in favor of William and Mary in 1688, the bishops tended to support James and hoped for an eventual Stuart restoration, which placed them in an odd position in regard to their prayer book. The 1662 book included, as had most of its predecessors, prayers for the monarch: but should these Jacobites pray for William and Mary, whom they considered to be usurpers?

Moreover, William—a Dutch Calvinist, bred from birth in the presbyterian model—liked the bishops little more than they liked him and formally decreed that the Scots Kirk be presbyterian in governance. This left episcopalians, as many as a third of Scots, rather out in the cold, and unsure how to organize their worship, especially their Eucharistic worship, which had been in Laud's Liturgy slightly different than the English order. Their solution was to come up with a series of pamphlets, known as the "wee bookies," printing the order of service. But liturgists are notoriously reluctant to settle on a single order if they are not forced to, and since the episcopal party was not the established church, they were free to fiddle as they pleased. Liturgically inclined clergy rummaged through church history and found a number of Eucharistic prayers and structures, especially in the Eastern churches, that Cranmer had not known or had rejected. As Charles Hefling has commented, Eucharistic worship in Scotland

> was not a static tradition. Whereas in England
> printers were obliged to see that their Prayer
> Books conformed to a standard text, no such
> regulation applied to Scottish Episcopalians, and
> there were never 'sealed books' to conform to,
> as there were for the 1662 Prayer Book. As time
> went on, the reprints began to vary, sometimes in
> their wording and sometimes in the arrangement
> of parts and paragraphs. By 1764, when the version that was to become the recognized standard

appeared, a number of interesting and significant alterations had accumulated.[3]

Scottish episcopalians had, on the whole inadvertently, created a library of worship possibilities, a set of liturgical modules.

It is at this point that the Scottish story joins the American one, largely through the complicated life of one Samuel Seabury. Seabury, born in 1729, was a Yale-educated Anglican priest from Connecticut, as his father had been before him, and had been made priest by an English bishop when he was visiting that country in 1753. Since ordination to the priesthood is in Anglicanism an episcopal office only, and there were no American bishops—the whole of North America having, oddly, been deemed part of the diocese of London—one had to travel to England to become a priest. (The elder Seabury had been made priest there in 1731, just a few years after the pathbreaking Samuel Johnson.) This situation became still more awkward when, after American independence, American Anglicans could no longer be part of the Church of England and therefore needed their own bishops. So when the Anglican clergy of Connecticut decided, in 1783, to name Samuel Seabury their bishop, he did what he had done when seeking ordination to the priesthood: he sailed to England.

One wonders what thoughts went through Seabury's mind during his passage. He may have expected a relatively warm reception, since in the years leading

up to the revolution he had been an outspoken royalist, the author of several pro-British pamphlets that
drew slashing retorts from Alexander Hamilton. But
he was now an American citizen, not a subject of the
king, and this proved an insurmountable obstacle for
the simple reason that ordination to the priesthood
or the episcopacy, or appointment to any public office in England, required the candidate to swear an
Oath of Supremacy, acknowledging the authority of
the British monarch—an oath almost identical to the
one Henry VIII had devised in 1534 and that Thomas
More had subsequently refused to sign, which led to
his imprisonment and execution. So Seabury could
only be consecrated as bishop by first renouncing
his American citizenship, which would also mean
renouncing the very episcopal office he had been
called to. This was a double bind indeed, and Seabury
evaded its grasp by heading north to Scotland.

The Scottish bishops, still supporters of the Stuart cause and no friends of the Hanoverian dynasty
holding the throne in London, would impose no
Oath of Supremacy. They were happy to consecrate
Seabury as a bishop. However, they imposed a condition. They insisted that when he returned to lead
the Anglicans of Connecticut, he would not use the
service of Holy Communion hallowed by the 1662
English *Book of Common Prayer*, but rather the form
that had emerged in Scotland after all those years of
experimentation in the "wee bookies." And so Seabury's consecration as the first American bishop set

America's Anglicans—henceforth known as Episcopalians—on the path toward a prayer book that
would differ in significant ways from the English
one. And that would in turn help create an environ-
ment in which Anglicans around the world, including in England itself, would think a great deal about
how the old and hard-won book might be made
something quite other than it had been.

Up to this time the Scottish situation with regard
to the prayer book had been seen by leaders of the
English church as an unfortunate but unavoidable
oddity, as was true with so much else in Scotland. But
now they were faced with the prospect of a future in
which their beloved *Book of Common Prayer* was but
one among many varieties—an especially daunting
thought as they contemplated the reach of the British Empire, now nearing its greatest point. Suddenly
it became possible to imagine very different prayer
books in Canada, India, Australia, South Africa, and
anywhere else in the Empire, even if those places had
not declared their independence and emancipated
themselves from British rule. This awareness essentially founds Anglicanism as an idea, and ever afterward shapes it as a reality.

In 1888, the third Lambeth Conference—a gathering
of Anglican bishops from throughout the world, a
gathering made necessary by the puzzle of this thing
called "Anglicanism"—passed a resolution articulat-

ing the bishops' core commitments. It was based on a resolution passed two years earlier by the Episcopalians in America when they gathered in Chicago, and it contained but four brief statements, so the formulation became known as the Chicago-Lambeth Quadrilateral. The statement had been promoted, and first drafted, by an American priest named William Reed Huntington, whose passion was to see Anglicans reunited with Catholic and Orthodox Christians: he called this "Home Reunion." (That this should become a widespread Anglican concern is perhaps surprising, and the reasons for it will soon be explored.) The version passed at Lambeth resolved that,

> in the opinion of this Conference, the following Articles supply a basis on which approach may be by God's blessing made towards Home Reunion:
>
> (a) The Holy Scriptures of the Old and New Testaments, as "containing all things necessary to salvation," and as being the rule and ultimate standard of faith.
>
> (b) The Apostles' Creed, as the Baptismal Symbol; and the Nicene Creed, as the sufficient statement of the Christian faith.
>
> (c) The two Sacraments ordained by Christ Himself—Baptism and the Supper of the Lord—ministered with unfailing use of Christ's Words of Institution, and of the elements ordained by Him.

(d) The Historic Episcopate, locally adapted
   in the methods of its administration to the
   varying needs of the nations and peoples
   called of God into the Unity of His Church.[4]

Note that there is no mention of the *Book of Common Prayer*. There had perhaps never been a church to which the motto *lex orandi, lex credendi*—the rule of prayer is the rule of belief—has been more applicable than the Church of England. Generations of its priests and laypersons took pride in having no Magisterium, no Canons of the Synod of Dort, no Westminster or Augsburg Confession, but just a prayer book that they all agreed to use. Nothing defined the Church of England more specifically or practically than use of the *Book of Common Prayer*. But in the Chicago-Lambeth Quadrilateral it is not mentioned as a necessary component of Anglicanism.

In large part this stems from the desire for Christian reunion, to which the imposition of a particular prayer book could only be an impediment. But it also constitutes an acknowledgment that both the contents and the use of prayer books—note the ominous plural—had already become highly variable in Anglican churches around the world and were sure to become still more varied in the future. In theory this is not problematic. According to the view articulated implicitly by Cranmer and with elaborate and logically powerful fullness by Richard Hooker half a century later, it was only necessary for *a given na-*

tion to have one book and one polity. Hooker was perfectly happy to concede to his Reformed counterparts that the episcopal model of church governance was not mandated by Scripture; however, he continued, neither was the presbyterian model. The Bible taught sound doctrine, but did not specify whether people were to be led by bishops or presbyters, nor whether hymns could be sung to musical accompaniment, nor what sequence of prayers should be said in church, nor how often they were to be said. Such questions were left to the discretion of particular bodies—in the case at hand, the established national Church of England, which had the authority to decree uniformity of belief and practice within its own orbit but not elsewhere. *Of course* other countries, perhaps even other dominions of the empire, could have their own prayer books.[5]

So, again in theory, there is no problem with this ever-increasing diversity of practice. But it was for the Church of England a destabilizing thought. It was a reminder that the prayer book could be other than it was, which was in turn a reminder of those times of social unrest, power struggles, succession controversies, and civil war that nineteenth-century Anglicans devoutly hoped were behind them forever. Rather than being a beacon set firmly on a peak for all to see and to navigate by, the prayer book became something contingent and historical, and therefore potentially unfinished. It is my contention that among the events that generated these destabilizing intellectual currents, the episcopal consecration of Samuel Seabury was an especially important one. From that point on, members of the Church of England knew they had cousins across the sea with a rather different *lex orandi*—a knowledge that has its curious formal acknowledgment a hundred years later in the absence of any reference to the *Book of Common Prayer* in the Chicago-Lambeth Quadrilateral.

📖

Between the consecration of Samuel Seabury and the Chicago-Lambeth Quadrilateral, as a kind of pivot point that ensured that the former would lead to the latter, stands the Tractarian movement—or the Oxford movement, or Anglo-Catholicism. Those may be three names for the same development, or three overlapping developments, but in either case it was made possible by this historicizing of the prayer book, and by scholarly tools that encouraged deeper exploration of Christian liturgical history. The same philological, archaeological, and paleographical energies that eventually resulted in the discovery of Troy and the decipherment of the Rosetta Stone also made possible one of the major events in the history of the *Book of Common Prayer*.

Thomas Cranmer's library at Croydon Palace may have been vast in its own time, but a Victorian historian of liturgy would have wept at its poverty. The great revolution in scholarship—the creation of the Republic of Letters—initiated by the early Renaissance and Reformation had just begun to gather momentum in Cranmer's time, though already people were beginning to complain that there were too many books to read and too much to know.[6] The proliferation of the "wee bookies" in Scotland would have happened in any event because of varying liturgical preferences but was accelerated by ongoing discoveries in the history of Christian worship. As the years and decades rolled past, the temporal and geographical range of scholars increased; they learned more and more about medieval English and continental practices, about the Eastern church, about the era of the Church Fathers, about the still longer history of Jewish worship. And the rise of the Tractarians gave the strongest impetus yet to this kind of study, which would have profound effects on the understanding and use of the prayer book.

John Henry Newman was the most controversial and the dominant figure of Victorian religious life, and a history of English religion or of Anglicanism would have to grant him a central role. In a biography of the *Book of Common Prayer* his place is not quite so high, in part because his influence in prayer-book controversies is oblique, hard to define, and not what it is commonly thought to be. People often imagine Newman to have been highly concerned with ritual, eager to follow the highest Roman liturgical practices, and therefore likely to have been deeply uncomfortable with the prayer book. But as long as Newman was an Anglican he defended the prayer book and followed its rubrics faithfully, without evident discomfort. It was the specifically *theological* claims of the Roman church that engaged him, and the more they did, the more concerned he became to determine whether, as a priest ordained in the Church of England, he could reconcile Catholic teaching with his profession of the Articles of Religion. As he explains in his great autobiography, *Apologia Pro Vita Sua*, for a long time be believed that he could, but eventually decided that he could not, at which point he left the English church and was received into the Roman one. But some years before this move, Newman had emerged as a strong defender of the prayer book, and the power of that defense would last within the Church of England, and beyond it, long after Newman had decamped for Rome.[7]

The Tractarians are so called because of the *Tracts for the Times* that Newman inaugurated in 1833 and contributed to and edited until 1841. In Tract 90 Newman attempted to show that the Articles of Religion were fundamentally compatible with Roman teaching; the resulting furor led to the suspension of the tracts, and Newman's giving up his places at Oxford—as a tutor at Oriel College and the vicar of the University Church of St. Mary the Virgin—for a period of retreat that would eventuate, in 1845, in his submission to Rome. But the early tracts were devoted to restoring specifically Anglican traditions that the writers felt had been neglected by evangelicals and Latitudinarians alike. It would be a great mistake to think that the Tractarians were equally opposed to both of those groups. From the moralistic and effectively deistic broad-church model they were thoroughly alienated, but they shared the fundamental goal of evangelicalism: the spiritual renewal of the English people. (It is significant that some of the most important figures in the high-church renewal of the Church of England, including Newman and John Mason Neale, were evangelicals before they were Anglo-Catholics.) However, the Tractarians believed that the evangelicals pursued this goal by wholly inadequate means, and that the evident waning of evangelical energy and influence in the first decades of the nineteenth century demonstrated this inadequacy. For Newman and his confederates, Whitefield's neglect of the traditional formal worship of the church in favor of a flamboyantly emotional and wholly word-based model of spirituality may have been effective in the short term, but in the long had been disastrous. Even Wesley's attachment to formal worship had been deficient; his followers were far more neglectful. The evangelicals, like some of the seeds in Jesus's parable of the sower, had sprung up quickly, but "when the sun was up, they were scorched; and because they had no root, they withered away" (Matthew 13:6). The "root" the evangelicals, and still more the Latitudinarians, had rejected, and that the Tractarians sought to rediscover, was to be found first in the *Book of Common Prayer*.

Thus Newman's Tract 3, "Thoughts Respectfully Addressed to the Clergy on Alterations in the Liturgy." His view on proposed changes to the prayer book may neatly be summed up: he was against changing "even one jot or tittle of it." Newman offers multiple reasons for refusing proposed changes, some of them merely practical, some of them moral and spiritual. He begins by noting that among the many who desire changes to the prayer book, few of them want the *same* changes: as had been the case since 1549, some sought to have a book that came closer to traditional Catholic practice, while others wanted briefer, simpler liturgies and more freedom for extemporaneous prayers. It would be impossible to satisfy one group without more deeply alienating the other. Newman also scorns those priests who would change the prayer book because laypersons desired it, since such servility is incompatible with what Newman believed to be the high calling of the priesthood: "Is this to bear about you the solemn office of a GUIDE and TEACHER in Israel, or to *follow a lead*?"[8]

But Newman's strongest and deepest warning resists what he calls "the temper of innovation"—the *disposition* to change. "A taste for criticism grows upon the mind," he points out. "When we begin to examine and take to pieces, our judgment becomes perplexed, and our feelings unsettled. I do not know whether others feel this to the same extent, but for myself, I confess there are few parts of the Service that I could not disturb myself about, and feel fastidious at, if I allowed my mind in this abuse of reason." One abuses one's reason by employing it to shine a critical light simply because one can, not because one must. And this "unsettling of the mind" is "a frightful thing; both to ourselves, and more so to our flocks. They have long regarded the Prayer Book with reverence as the stay of their faith and devotion. The weaker sort it will make sceptical; the better it will offend and pain." The long stability of the prayer book, and the "reverence" generated by that stability, are great and certain goods, which would be lost by taking the mere chance of improvement. "Be prepared then," he exhorts his fellow clergy, "for petitioning against any alterations in the Prayer Book which may be proposed."

The ruling convictions here are, in one of the best senses of the word, conservative, and Newman felt that conservatism with his whole being. His urgency in this matter was contagious, and he and his fellow Tractarians led a powerful renewal of prayer-book worship in England. Priests who had conducted Morning and Evening Prayer as infrequently as possible now exhorted their parishioners to follow the daily practices that Cranmer had thought so central. Choral Evensong became a popular service, and not just in cathedrals and college chapels. More crucially, Holy Communion began to be offered far more frequently in parishes across England and eventually, as the Tractarian movement spread its influence, in other parts of the Anglican world. On Easter day 1800, one Communion service was offered at St. Paul's Cathedral in London, with six communicants.

Seventy-five years later, it had become common for ordinary parish churches to offer Communion weekly—in some churches even daily. When one considers that these changes were accompanied by a dramatic rise in church attendance in the first three-quarters of the nineteenth century, it seems likely that the Victorian era was the high tide of prayer-book worship. More Anglicans than at any other point in history knew the book, possessed their own copies of the book, heard its words spoken regularly, ingested those words. It is telling that in the late nineteenth century the Cunard cruise line and Boots the Chemist arranged to have editions of the *Book of Common Prayer* printed with their own company imprint prominently displayed thereupon.[9]

The Boots the Chemist prayer book is telling in more ways than one. It testifies to a culture saturated with the Anglican liturgy, but from the specifically Christian point of view that saturation is an ambiguous achievement. People with little or no Christian belief could be just as determined to conserve the prayer book as Newman was. Thus Matthew Arnold argued that the prayer book "has created sentiments deeper than we can see or measure. Our feeling does not connect itself with any language about righteousness and religion, but with that language." But this does not mean that we believe the prayer book's teachings in any traditional way: "Of course, those who can take them literally will still continue to use them. But for us also, who can no longer put the literal meaning on them which others do, and which we ourselves once did, they retain a power, and something in us vibrates to them." Arnold thinks this appropriate, since "these old forms of expression were men's sincere attempt to set forth with due honour what we honour also"; therefore "we can *feel*" the doctrines of the prayer book, "even when we no longer take them literally."[10]

Newman and his confederates would have found approval on these grounds simply appalling; again, the primary consideration in Newman's mind was always theological truth, along with the adequacy of any given religious language to express it. Arnold's "feelings" could not have been less to the point. It was for similar reasons that many of the Tractarians came to regret Anglican establishment, believing it restrained the church's prophetic function. Establishment was incompatible with the proper independence of theological judgment and fearless preaching. Those who felt the most strongly about this wanted to omit a particular set of prayers from the prayer book: the so-called State Prayers, most of which had been added in 1662, which commemorate King Charles as a martyr, pray for the current sovereign, denounce the Gunpowder Plot of 1605, and so on. Resistance to these prayers gained some of the Anglo-Catholics a reputation for deficient patriotism that many of them were happy to bear.

But the Church of England *was* established, and therefore entangled in multiple ways with the state,

and as the nineteenth century wore on those entanglements became more fraught and tense. One
of the better-known ecclesiastical controversies of
the Victorian era concerned a priest named George
Cornelius Gorham, whose bishop believed that his
views about baptism were outside the parameters of
the Articles of Religion and on those grounds denied
him a post. Gorham mounted a legal challenge that
ended up being adjudicated by the Judicial Committee of the Privy Council, which in 1850 granted him
the place the bishop had denied him. This upset the
Anglo-Catholics deeply, even though—or perhaps
because—the committee offered what they called a
"neutral reading" of the baptismal theology of the
articles as "more congenial with the existing and traditional sentiments of the English people." Newman
replied scathingly, and unfairly, that the whole situation demonstrated that "neither does English law
seek justice, nor English religion seek truth."[11]

What the situation in fact demonstrated was,
first, the complexities generated by having a church
established in such a way that laymen employed by
the government could have final say in church affairs, and second, the tendency of these complexities to gather around the interpretation of the prayer
book. The Judicial Committee's "neutral reading"
was, effectively, a plea that everyone just get along,
and get along by vowing obedience to the *Book of
Common Prayer* while allowing one another a good
deal of freedom to read that book according to theo-

logical preference. The members of the committee were not saying that Gorham's interpretation of the prayer book's teaching on baptism was superior to the bishop's, but rather that the bishop was ruling too narrowly and should have made more room for theological variance. They did not believe that every minister should be Latitudinarian, but they did, it seems, believe the boundaries of the Church of England as a whole needed to be set as broadly as possible.

In taking this position, the Judicial Committee was effectively embodying the views of one of the most notable Anglicans of their time, F. D. Maurice. For those who admire him—including perhaps most notably Horton Davies, the great historian of *Worship and Theology in England*—Maurice is something like the ideal Anglican, largely because of his refusal to accept the limitations, and indeed the falsifications, inherent in any theological partisanship. Maurice gave a reasonably clear description of his position in an open letter of 1841 to Samuel Wilberforce, son of the great abolitionist William Wilberforce and at the time archdeacon of Ripon, though later to be famous as the Bishop of Oxford and the debating opponent of Thomas Henry Huxley. To Archdeacon Wilberforce Maurice wrote, "I turn to the purely Protestant or Evangelical school, and I find its members working hard to explain away the meaning of our Catholic formularies." Such willful blindness to the manifest contents of the prayer book made Maurice unwilling to join the low-church, or evangelical, party. But "I turn again to the Catholic school. I find the most accomplished and logical of its members working hard to explain away the meaning of that formulary which the Reformation bequeathed to us, and in which the Protestantism of that age is, as I and most other persons believe, embodied."[12] This very different blindness rules out the high-church party as well. Although Maurice does not say so in the letter to Wilberforce, he also mistrusted the broad-church party for what he saw as its willingness to set almost *all* of the teachings of the prayer book, Reformed and Catholic alike, aside in favor of an insipid moralism.

What did Maurice suggest as an alternative to the choice among parties? The title of Horton Davies's chapter on Maurice offers a clear summary: "F. D. Maurice and the Liturgy as the Symbol of Unity in Church and State." Maurice saw social and spiritual unity as stemming from a shared obedience, a shared commitment to active lives of worship, a willingness to submit to the authority of a prayer book that somehow held together what one affirmed with all one's heart and what one deeply mistrusted. An old saying about God, often attributed to St. Ephrem the Syrian, goes, "This also is Thou; neither is this Thou." For Maurice, the prayer book itself possessed just such a mystical evasiveness, a resistance to explanatory categories. He wanted his fellow Anglicans to trust the book more than they trusted their own preferences and parties, to plunge into its depths to trust God to guide them through.

Presented thus, Maurice may seem an appealingly irenic thinker, but as Davies freely acknowledges, his influence was in his own time limited by his maddening obscurity of style, and he is largely forgotten today. Maurice tried so hard to avoid saying things that would place him within a party that it is often difficult to understand what he is saying at all. Consider this passage on the Eucharistic elements:

> But are we investing bread and wine with some magical properties? Are we supposing that they admit us into a Presence, which but for them would be far from us? Do they not rather bear witness, by their simplicity, by their universality, that it is *always* near to us, near to every one? Do they not say, "Will you live, move, have your being, in God, and yet be practically at a distance from Him, because you will not let Him approach you, enter into converse with you, subdue you?" Shall all this Love be about us day by day, and shall we be living, shut out from its power and influence, in a region of ice?
>
> Do you answer, "But may not many have enjoyed this Presence, may not many enjoy it now, who do not taste the elements?"
>
> Believe, and give thanks, that it is so. Acknowledge with hearty delight every fruit of God's Spirit, which you see in any person, who rejects

every Christian ordinance. Canvass it not, try not to make out that it is unreal, lest you blaspheme the Holy Ghost. Prize this Sacrament as the witness, the deepest, truest, simplest witness, that God is with men, that all good things are from Him, that nothing can be true in us but what is the reflection of His Truth.[13]

So the Sacrament is not magical, but neither is it unreal, and while the experience of God that we have in it is not unique, neither is it to be set aside lest we blaspheme. This also is the true meaning of the Sacrament, neither is this the true meaning of the Sacrament. Maurice habitually writes in this teasing, evasive manner, his chief communication being the incommunicability of the encounter with God that he enjoins everyone to have by going to church and submitting to the power of the prayer-book liturgy. His love of the prayer book and his belief in its inspired character are remarkable, but he would perhaps have done better merely to point at churches.

📖

Meanwhile, the parties' debates continued, largely because the party members saw Maurice's position as functionally indistinguishable from Arnold's: to them it seemed to purchase social unity at the cost of truthfulness. Striving to concern themselves *only* with truth, Newman and the other first-generation Anglo-Catholics prompted, whether intentionally or not, a vast cadre of priests and scholars who sought to prove not just that the Articles of Religion were compatible with traditional Roman practices but also that the whole of the prayer book—including most particularly its rubrics—was as well. England had seen little to compare with the passion of the subsequent debates since Puritans ripped the Communion rails from Laud's churches and made bonfires with them. The Anglo-Catholic controversy rarely achieved quite those levels of intensity, but priests did end up in jail when they would neither recant, nor refrain from enacting, their preferences in candlesticks. And that is a remarkable thing.

In a seminal essay published in 1995, the theologian William Cavanaugh set out to refute the common belief that the great wars of the pre-Enlightenment period were wars of religion; rather, he contends, they arose from the creation of, and were fought to defend, the modern nation-state.[14] In Cavanaugh's compelling repudiation of conventional wisdom, the early modern period was largely devoted to a partitioning of the human person for purposes of assigning its control. Throughout most of Europe, church and state reached a compromise according to which the care of souls belongs to the former and the care of bodies to the latter. Churches had to content themselves with shaping thought and worship while ceding legal authority over acts done with the body to states. This led to the shrinking or elimination of canon law and of practices that had gone back to the early decades of Christendom, when a bishop like Augustine of Hippo devoted much of his time to settling legal disputes among members of his congregation. From the early modern period on the state would be in charge of bodies and objects.

But England is the great exception to this rule, though it was affected in profound ways by the continent-wide changes, because it maintained an established church. This meant that the church was still concerned with bodies, still had charge over bodies, as could be seen in those fierce debates between Cranmer and John Knox that led to the creation of the Black Rubric. To the established church, the state-church or church-state, was given the task of fixing the status of kneeling during the taking of Communion. A bodily posture had to be declared forbidden, or obligatory, or optional. (In theological language, optional acts are *adiaphora*, or "things indifferent.") About control of their bodies people can become particularly agitated, thus the burning of the Communion rails when Laud fell and the church could no longer command those receiving the Sacrament to kneel. Similarly, powerful associations can attach themselves to familiar objects in a church, as John Betjeman noted in the 1950s in a passage notable both for its psychological acuity and its class snobbery:

> The reader who casts his mind back to his early worship as a child will remember that a hymn board, or a brass cross or a garish window were,

from his customary gazing on them Sunday after Sunday, part of his religious life. If as an older and more informed person his taste and knowledge tell him these things are cheap and hideous, he will still regret their passing with a part of him that is neither his intellect nor his learning. How much more will an uninformed villager, whose feeling always runs higher where the church is concerned than a townsman's, cling to those objects he has known as a boy, however cheap they are.[15]

Thus the power of candlestick placement to capture the public imagination in a way that disputations over the meaning of the prayer book's theology of Baptism never could. The Gorham case was a cause célèbre among the ordained, whose sources of authority were in dispute, but not among ordinary laypersons.

The rubrics of the prayer book matter so much, then, because they decree what may or may not be done with *bodies* and *objects*. And in the middle of the Victorian era the interpretation of one rubric in particular became the focal point for profound conflict within the Church of England and across the whole of society. It is called the Ornaments Rubric, and it first appeared in the Elizabethan *Book of Common Prayer* of 1559. In the eighteenth century, the lowest of low-church eras, it was thought sufficiently trivial that it was omitted from many editions; but a hundred years later everything vital seemed to hinge on it. It appears as a kind of preface to the service of Morning Prayer, and reads as follows:

> *The Morning and Evening Prayer shall be used in the accustomed Place of the Church, Chapel, or Chancel; except it shall be otherwise determined by the Ordinary of the Place. And the Chancels shalt remain as they have done in times past.*
>
> *And here is to be noted, that such Ornaments of the Church, and of the Ministers thereof, at all Times of their Ministration, shall be retained, and be in use, as were in this Church of England, by the Authority of Parliament, in the Second Year of the Reign of King Edward the Sixth.*

This rubric governs what objects may furnish a church—above all its Communion table—and what priests may place on their bodies. In its original Elizabethan context, it was meant to resist Puritan attempts to outlaw anything that might make the Lord's Table look like an altar, and any form of distinctly clerical dress, but at the same time sought to avoid the appearance of popery. It is often thought that were it not for the traditionalist preferences of Elizabeth herself the Puritans would have had their way, but instead a compromise was reached that, like so many of the prayer-book compromises over the centuries, seems to have left everyone somewhat unhappy. The stricter Reformers hated to see a highly decorated table and a minister wearing even something as unusual as a surplice—given their commitment to "the priesthood of all believers" they thought ministers should dress as other congregants did—but traditionalists grieved to be denied a stone altar and priests garbed in albs, chasubles, and copes.

But from the vantage point of 1845 or thereabouts, the details of the rubric were a bit fuzzy. What precisely *were* the ornaments "in use . . . in the Second Year of the Reign of King Edward the Sixth," that is, in 1549? To this difficult question a number of clerical members of the Republic of Letters devoted their fullest energies. Chief among these was not Newman, nor any other of the Oxford men who are typically seen as leaders of this movement, but a Cambridge man named John Mason Neale. (He is now best known for his many hymns and carols, including "All Glory, Laud, and Honor," "Good King Wenceslas," and the translation from Latin of "O Come, O Come, Emmanuel.") To Neale, Newman and his friends had been focused too exclusively on questions of theological truth. As he wrote to a friend in 1844, "It is clear to me that the Tract writers missed one great principle, namely that of Aesthetics, and it is unworthy of them to blind themselves to it."[16]

Neale was born in 1818, seventeen years after Newman, and by the time he came to study at Cambridge the *Tracts for the Times* were well underway; he came to theological and spiritual maturity under their influence. In 1839, when still undergraduates, he and some friends cofounded the Cambridge Camden Society in order to foster "the study of Gothic Architecture, and of Ecclesiastical Antiques." A few years later it was renamed the Ecclesiological Society, and in 1848 it published a volume titled *Hierurgia Anglicana*. It is not clear how much of the book is Neale's own work, though it seems likely that he was responsible for much of it, and certainly he wrote its preface. Neale and his collaborators saw quite clearly that the Ornaments Rubric was key to the aesthetic renewal of the liturgy—which he believed to be key to its spiritual effect on Christians—and the *Hierurgia Anglicana* amounts to an archaeological unearthing of what churches had looked like and what priests had worn during King Edward's reign.

The tone of Neale's preface is bold, not to say aggressive. He forthrightly acknowledges that the Ornaments Rubric has been the source of controversy: "Much of late has been said and written about this rubrick, to the effect that English Churchmen cannot much longer consent to its violation." Moreover, he agrees that it has often been violated. But, in a neat application of rhetorical jujitsu, he claims that the Puritans, evangelicals, and Latitudinarians have been the ones doing the violating. The historical evidence shows, he claims, that the English church in the second year of Edward VI's reign employed ceremonial practices that placed them in clear continuity with the Roman church, the churches of Eastern Christendom, and the Patristic era. Why, then, he asks, "have none of our clergy and churchwardens determined at all risks, to fulfill their official obligations in this behalf?" Why have we not been faithful to our tradition and to the rubrics of the *Book of Common Prayer*?

The answer, Neale contends, lies in a combination of ignorance and arrogance. He particularly chastises bishops, to whom clergy and laypersons alike appealed when they spotted what they believed to be violations of the prayer book's instructions. "The Bishop does not know the rubric; or reads it as it is fashionable to read the Baptismal Office, by the rule of contrary: or, which is commonest of all, he claims to be superior to the rubric." The purpose of the *Hierurgia Anglicana* was to eliminate the ignorance and make the arrogance more difficult to sustain—and all in the name of obedience to the *Book of Common Prayer*.[17]

The evidences compiled in the *Hierurgia* were wildly exciting to the Anglo-Catholics. Anglican priests may not have worn chasubles since the reign of Queen Mary, but Neale started wearing one in 1850—and promptly got into trouble with his bishop for doing so. (Historical lessons, like most others, tend to be learned slowly.) If the record suggested that Cranmer tolerated stone altars and chancels separated from naves by rood screens, then the Victorians could build stone altars in their new Gothic churches. By doing so, they were only being faithful Anglicans, and more faithful, if it came to that, than the low churchmen and broad churchmen who were made apoplectic by such arrant popery. As it happened, Neale was unsympathetic to Rome; he greatly admired the Eastern churches and devoted much of his scholarly research in the remainder of his short life (he died at forty-eight) to writing about them, because they had retained patristic traditions without introducing what he believed to be the late and corrupt innovation of the papacy. When Newman went over, Neale wrote letter after letter encouraging his fellow Anglo-Catholics to stay the course. But many Anglicans, clerical and lay alike, entered the neo-Gothic churches built under the guidance of the Ecclesiological Society, saw the rood screens, smelled the incense, heard the chancel choirs chanting plainsong, and shuddered with alienation. This was not Anglicanism as they knew it and as their fathers had known it. It seemed to them that Catholicism—so long relegated to the margins of English society, so recently allowed to take a more public place—had won after all.

📖

For the rest of the nineteenth century, the Church of England was riven by conflicts generated by these varying interpretations of the Ornaments Rubric. In some cases, when the laity either got ahead of or lagged behind the liturgical positions of their vicars, actual riots ensued. Eventually, Archibald Campbell Tait, the Archbishop of Canterbury, introduced a bill to Parliament that would set limits on the Catholicizing of liturgy and church architecture. (Queen Victoria and her favorite minister, Benjamin Disraeli, were enthusiastic about the bill, but the devoted churchman William Ewart Gladstone lamented the transforming of the church's "liturgy into a parliamentary football"—perhaps the first use of that now worn-smooth phrase.[18]) The Public Worship Regulation Act became law in 1874 and over the next few decades resulted in the prosecution and conviction of several priests for elevating the Host during the prayer of consecration, mixing water with the Communion wine, and placing lighted candles in inappropriate places. Such prosecutions were deeply unpopular and ceased in the early twentieth century, though the act itself was not repealed until 1965.

The greatest influence of the Ecclesiological Society was in church architecture, which was Neale's deepest passion. He and his friends fervently believed that a certain period of the High Gothic marked the summit of church architecture, the very perfection of the making of sacred spaces, and that any deviation from that model weakened the spiritual power of Christian worship. For decades, members of the society devoted themselves most assiduously to the policing of church architecture, protesting and seeking revision of plans for new churches that they found deficient, mandating sweeping corrective restorations of old churches. They were utterly intolerant of architectural heresy. Their power grew vast, and not just in England. In the United States, for example, though Anglican churches on the East Coast tend even now to follow low-church practices established in the seventeenth century, the upper Midwest is full of Anglican parishes established in the mid- to late nineteenth century by Anglo-Catholics. One of the most resolutely Anglo-Catholic seminaries anywhere is Nashotah House, in southern Wisconsin, which opened its doors in 1842, and many Episcopalians in Chicago worship in Gothic buildings with baldachins over their altars and slippered priests bearing thurifers. It is slightly discomfiting to reflect that these models of Anglican worship developed because Elizabeth I would not allow the Puritans to prohibit all ceremonial and because a nineteenth-century English enthusiast for the Gothic rummaged around until he found evidence for high ritual being practiced in 1549. Yet so it is.

Neale's Ritualist movement, and the Tractarianism that preceded and laid the groundwork for it, had begun in reverence for the *Book of Common Prayer*. Newman argued that the prayer book be left unchanged and followed faithfully; Neale defended his liturgical and architectural preferences as perfectly obedient to the Ornaments Rubric. And as we have seen, their efforts did indeed lead to a renewal of interest in and commitment to the prayer book. But with their relentless focus on bodies and objects as symbolic conveyors of spiritual truth—their insistence on what Neale called the Sacramentalist principle that by "the outward and visible form, is signified something inward and spiritual: that the material fabrick symbolizes, embodies, figures, represents, expresses, answers to, some abstract meaning"[19]—they limited the words of the prayer book to an ancillary role. This limitation was reinforced by the Anglo-Catholic preference for sung services whenever they were possible—sung Eucharists and Evensongs especially, which allow the specific language of the prayers to disappear into a sensuous impressionism constructed primarily through architecture, incense, vestments, and melody. (Thus the line attributed to various rebellious Anglicans, most commonly to the twentieth-century American bishop James Pike: "I can sing the Creed, but I can't say it.")

All this was done in professed and usually genuine obedience to the Ornaments Rubric, but the practices nevertheless can feel quite distant from Cranmer's belief in the power of words to convey theological truth, and his consequent insistence that priests should enunciate their prayers clearly and "in a loud voice." The auditory churches of the Restoration era did much to capture this impulse, even as they neglected much of the ceremonial power of the pre-Reformation church, but in justifiably seeking to restore those ceremonies, the Ritualists may have erred in the opposite direction. They transformed Cranmer's powerful words into a kind of ambient music, often heard without acknowledgment, received aesthetically but not necessarily with the ear of understanding.

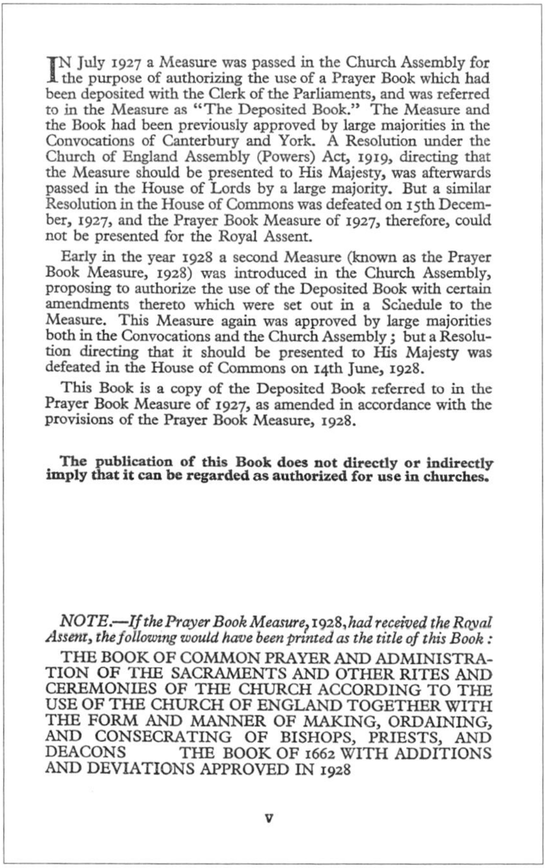

IN July 1927 a Measure was passed in the Church Assembly for the purpose of authorizing the use of a Prayer Book which had been deposited with the Clerk of the Parliaments, and was referred to in the Measure as "The Deposited Book." The Measure and the Book had been previously approved by large majorities in the Convocations of Canterbury and York. A Resolution under the Church of England Assembly (Powers) Act, 1919, directing that the Measure should be presented to His Majesty, was afterwards passed in the House of Lords by a large majority. But a similar Resolution in the House of Commons was defeated on 15th December, 1927, and the Prayer Book Measure of 1927, therefore, could not be presented for the Royal Assent.

Early in the year 1928 a second Measure (known as the Prayer Book Measure, 1928) was introduced in the Church Assembly, proposing to authorize the use of the Deposited Book with certain amendments thereto which were set out in a Schedule to the Measure. This Measure again was approved by large majorities both in the Convocations and the Church Assembly ; but a Resolution directing that it should be presented to His Majesty was defeated in the House of Commons on 14th June, 1928.

This Book is a copy of the Deposited Book referred to in the Prayer Book Measure of 1927, as amended in accordance with the provisions of the Prayer Book Measure, 1928.

The publication of this Book does not directly or indirectly imply that it can be regarded as authorized for use in churches.

NOTE.—If the Prayer Book Measure, 1928, had received the Royal Assent, the following would have been printed as the title of this Book :

THE BOOK OF COMMON PRAYER AND ADMINISTRATION OF THE SACRAMENTS AND OTHER RITES AND CEREMONIES OF THE CHURCH ACCORDING TO THE USE OF THE CHURCH OF ENGLAND TOGETHER WITH THE FORM AND MANNER OF MAKING, ORDAINING, AND CONSECRATING OF BISHOPS, PRIESTS, AND DEACONS   THE BOOK OF 1662 WITH ADDITIONS AND DEVIATIONS APPROVED IN 1928

v

FIGURE 6. Although the revision of the *Book of Common Prayer* presented to Parliament in 1928 was voted down, copies were printed for some decades afterward with the melancholy explanation seen here.

The Book of Common Prayer with the Addition and Deviations Proposed in 1928 (Oxford University Press). Collection of the author.

The Pressures of the Modern

CHAPTER 6

As the Victorian era drew to a close, the *Book of Common Prayer* was at or near the height of its career, something that was widely understood at the time. Even as early as 1865, in a scholarly edition of the prayer book, the Reverends W. M. Campion and W. J. Beamont note that "probably at no period, since the Reformation, has the national Church occupied the attention of intelligent men in foreign lands and of all classes in our own land, to so large an extent as she does at the present day"—a situation for which much of the credit is due to the *Book of Common Prayer*. Nor did the editors see any need to revise their judgment as their book went through multiple editions throughout the rest of the nineteenth and into the twentieth century. However, the editors continue, their beloved Church of England is simultaneously undergoing harsh judgment. "On the one hand she has been assailed as inclining too much to the practices and doctrines of the Church of Rome; on the other as having too little sympathy with the primitive usages of Christianity. In each of these cases her Prayer-book is made the chief object of attack." The very same book that makes the chief contribution to the influence of the Anglican way also draws the greatest enmity.[1]

Campion and Beamont seem to intuit that the very forces that had propelled the prayer book to such a height of respect and influence had also prepared the way for great changes. I have argued that the most powerful of these forces was Anglo-Catholicism and its allied movements, which had devoted massive scholarly energies to the unearthing of liturgical history. That history, once thoroughly uncovered, did less to confirm the perfection of the prayer book than to show all the ways in which it might have been, and still could be, other. In Tract 3 Newman had warned of the dangers of a "temper of innovation," but by the end of the nineteenth century researchers like those of the Ecclesiological Society had provided people with such a rich history of liturgical practices—so many delectable options— that it was impossible for any serious liturgist not to imagine revisions.

In the United States in particular, without the external restraints imposed by establishment, those revisions could proceed at whatever pace the worshipping communities would tolerate. Consider what happened after the adoption of the first American *Book of Common Prayer* in 1789:

In 1792 the General Convention [of the Protestant Episcopal Church in the United States] adopted revised ordination rites; in 1799, a rite for the consecration of a church; in 1801, a slightly revised version of the Articles of Religion. The convention of 1804 added a rite for the institution of ministers, and a prayer for conventions was officially added among the occasional prayers in 1835. . . . Other minor changes were made in 1808, 1832, 1835, 1838, 1841, and 1868.[2]

All this in preparation for a thorough (but in most respects quite conservative) reworking of the whole book in 1892. Meanwhile, Anglicans in Ireland showed their discomfort with the Catholicizing tendencies across the Irish Sea by revising their version of the *Book of Common Prayer* in an evangelical direction in 1877, while momentum for liturgical revision in the opposite direction began to build in Canada.

Throughout the English-speaking world, the possibilities of revision urged themselves on priests, scholars, and laypersons. And though the scholarly stimulus of Anglo-Catholicism played a major role, so too did changes in the English language, which had gradually rendered much prayer-book language unfamiliar, along with the language of the King James Bible. As daily speech moved further from the norms of the sixteenth and seventeenth centuries, those two great texts became simultaneously harder to understand and more venerable: stateliness, formality, and peculiarity of diction and vocabulary combined to make the books seem holy and tampering with them a profanation. Thus when a group of scholars took up the task of revising the Authorized Version of the Bible in 1879, they felt obliged to pledge that their revision would be as minimal as possible: they wished to "adapt King James' version to the present state of the English language without changing the idiom and vocabulary." In the end they felt they could only make corrections to obvious errors in the old translation.

Likewise, many who supported revision of the prayer book did so reluctantly; they loved the old language but saw that it was increasingly subject to misunderstanding. Take for example the great General Confession from the service of Holy Communion, in which,

> We acknowledge and bewail our manifold sins and wickedness, which we, from time to time, most grievously have committed, by thought, word, and deed, against thy Divine Majesty, provoking most justly thy wrath and indignation against us. We do earnestly repent, and are heartily sorry for these our misdoings; the remembrance of them is grievous unto us; The burden of them is intolerable.[3]

Let us set aside, for the moment, those who would seek to revise this passage on theological grounds—

though we shall return to them later—and focus for a moment on the language. One of the terms most likely to be misunderstood here is the last one quoted, "intolerable": that word now largely conveys a sense of injustice or unfairness, so that a modern person who says that "the burden of [my sins] is intolerable" may well feel like a liar or pretender. But Cranmer's language does not refer to what one senses, but to the condition one is actually in. The Latin root lies close to the surface: "intolerable" simply means "too heavy to be carried." The theological statement is, within the wide scope of Christian orthodoxy, unremarkable and unexceptionable: I cannot carry my sins, so Christ must carry them for me.

The same problem arises with the Exhortation that precedes the Communion proper, during which would-be communicants are reminded of Jesus Christ, "who did humble himself, even to the death upon the Cross, for us, miserable sinners, who lay in darkness and the shadow of death; that he might make us the children of God, and exalt us to everlasting life." Few people feel at any given moment as though they are indeed "miserable sinners," and to modern ears the phrase sounds unhealthily self-lacerating, but as with "intolerable," the Latin original clarifies. "Miserable" is derived from *miseria*—the familiar liturgical phrase *miserere me, Domine* means "have mercy on me, Lord"—so a "miserable sinner" is simply "a sinner in need of mercy." Again, what now may be taken as a cue for feeling was meant simply as a statement of theological fact, an announcement of human beings' position in relation to God.[4]

All this is easily enough explained, but there are dozens, if not hundreds, of such trip wires in the prayer book, and a pastor could not reasonably be expected to find ways to explain them all. Likewise, people attending services could not reasonably be expected to be present at any given venue in which their pastors would do such explaining. Increasingly, then, ordinary people were alienated from the prayer book by long, slow historical forces that could not be arrested. More and more leaders of the Church of England came around to the idea that venerability would have to be sacrificed to the greater need of comprehension.

In 1904, the then recently-installed Archbishop of Canterbury, Randall Davidson, responding both the persistent popularity of Anglo-Catholicism and the equally persistent resistance to it, had commissioned an evaluation of the state of church discipline. In 1906 the Report of the Royal Commission on Ecclesiastical Discipline announced that violations of the Ornaments Rubric and other policies happened regularly. However, the commission did not recommend a renewal of the recently ceased prosecutions, but rather a broadening of the rubrics. "The law of public worship in the Church of England is too narrow for the religious life of the present generation. It needlessly condemns much which a great section of

Church people, including some of her most devoted members, value; and modern thought and feeling are characterized by a care of ceremonial, a sense of dignity in worship, and an appreciation of the continuity of the Church, which were not similarly felt when the law took its present shape."[5] It was on these grounds that a revision of the *Book of Common Prayer* was envisioned: narrow grounds, focusing mainly on the rubrics. And so scholars set to work, sifting through the possibilities for modest change.

But long before they had finished, an event occurred that made it absolutely necessary for the Church of England to confront the challenge of a more substantive revision. That event was World War I.

📖

The century from Napoleon's defeat at Waterloo in June 1815 to the assassination of Archduke Franz Ferdinand in June 1914 was perhaps the most peaceful in European history, and it is difficult to overstress the psychic shock generated by the return of war to the continent.[6]

One of the recurrent themes of the literature of the Great War is the ironic contrast between the long-standing habits and practices of English society and the blunt horrors of the battlefield. The beautiful language of the prayer book clashes dissonantly with the soldiers' experience. Vera Brittain, in her memoir *Testament of Youth*, describes the funeral of a young soldier named Victor, a close friend of her fiancé, Roland, who had already been killed at the front:

> Five days later Victor was buried at Hove. No place on earth could have been more ironically inappropriate for a military funeral than that secure, residential town, I reflected, as I listened with rebellious anger to the calm voice of the local clergyman intoning the prayers:
>
>> "Grant, we beseech Thee, O Lord, Thine Eternal Rest to all those who have died for their country, as this our brother hath; and grant that we may so follow his good example that we may be united with him in Thine Everlasting Kingdom."
>
> Eternal Rest, I reflected, had been the last thing that Victor wanted; he had told me so himself.[7]

Brittain was a nurse during much of the war, and she complains that the profession of nursing was too hedged about with a sense of "sanctity," which is marked by the nunlike uniforms the nurses—called "Sisters"—wore and by their strict adherence to the rhythms of Morning and Evening Prayer. To Brittain it is all too "Victorian"; already, thirty years after Victoria's death, the term is strongly pejorative.[8]

In another classic memoir of the Great War, *Good-Bye to All That*, Robert Graves describes coming home on leave in 1916 and being pressured by his parents to attend multiple Good Friday services.

"My father wanted me to attend the early morning service, and even tried to bully me into it, but I was owed thirteen months' sleep; and though he came hobbling along to my bedroom door at half-past six, banging loudly and saying that my mother counted on my accompanying her on this day of all days, I did not turn out."[9]

But despite his being sick, exhausted, and recovering from war injuries, Graves could not escape the later service: "Then down came my mother with her prayer-book, veil and deep religious look, and I could not spoil the day for her." He attended the rite, but found its length interminable and the clergyman obnoxious, "bellowing about the Glurious Perfurmances of our Surns and Brethren in Frunce today." Graves passed the time by composing anticlerical Latin epigrams in his head, and when the service was over—followed by a painful return home, "the dreary push up-hill, my mother helping me, my father holding the prayer-book, myself sweating like a bull"—he never attended another one. (But he continued to use a verse from Psalm 121—"I will lift up mine eyes unto the hills, from whence cometh my help"—as a "charm against trouble.")

The prayer book, then, becomes a synecdoche for English society in time of war: civilian incomprehension of the war's miseries illustrated through an ongoing sanctimonious recital of the Cranmerian cadences. The intrinsically repetitive character of liturgy reinforces the feeling of mindlessness, of saying without thinking, and the prayer book's fixed place in the Establishment connects it with vast, pitiless, institutional forces—forces that blithely send young men to their deaths.[10] And this was not just a problem among the highly educated, like Brittain and Graves; many priests who served as chaplains during the war reported that the illiterate, or barely literate, foot soldiers they were charged to serve could make no sense of sixteenth-century diction and syntax, and were therefore left uncomforted in their time of need.

The lamentations of these chaplains reinforced, in an odd way, arguments the most ritualistic Anglo-Catholics had been making for several decades. One of the most commendable, and least-known, features of Anglo-Catholicism is its powerful social conscience: inheritors of the Tractarian legacy had devoted themselves to ministry in the worst slums in England's cities—places largely or wholly neglected by the Church of England in any of its manifestations—where they built churches, schools, and social centers. These priests were like missionaries in their own land, and they too had seen the prayer book's inability to reach whole swaths of the English people. In their view, as Alec Vidler has summed it up,

The conventional worship of the Church of England was too dull and cold and reserved to appeal to, or to mean much to, people living in those conditions. Anyhow they were people who could learn much more through the eye than through the ear. It was common sense to bring home to them the meaning of the Church and sacraments through every artifice of colour, music, and dramatic action.[11]

Of course, priests of this disposition served in the trenches of the Great War as well, and this provided many opportunities for them to advocate for practices often thought Romish: the absence of prayers for the dead from the prayer book was, not surprisingly, a particular concern of theirs. (They also believed that the exigencies of wartime proved the wisdom of the Roman practice—long forbidden in Anglicanism—of reserving the Sacrament. Many who would never have endorsed such a thing in peacetime agreed with them about that.) But chaplains who came from different traditions, while seeing the same problems, sought different solutions: not the elevation of the forms of worship, which would in any case have been impossible on the front, but the simplification and modernization of the language of the *Book of Common Prayer*. One group of theologically liberal chaplains said bluntly that the usual prayer-book services—especially Morning and Evening Prayer, with their strong, some might say relentless, penitential tone—were "uninstructive and misleading to some, irritating and alienating to others."[12] Thomas Cranmer's great project had come to seem inadequate from a number of different perspectives. The few minor adjustments, primarily to a handful of rubrics, that had seemed sufficient in 1906, now seemed woefully inadequate. Work on a more significant revision therefore began to accelerate.

The chaplains' desire—and that of many others as well—for a simplified, linguistically modernized, and theologically less intimidating prayer book was a strong goad to revision. But once the actual work began, the chaplains' pleas "fell on deaf ears and liturgical revision proceeded on academic and party lines."[13] Multiple forces converged to make impossible the kind of revision the chaplains hoped for. As has already been noted, one important source of resistance was the air of timeless sanctity that had come to surround both the prayer book and the King James Bible. Already by the mid-nineteenth century people had begun to speak contemptuously of "thees and thous," but for every person frustrated by such language there were perhaps several others who felt that such formal language was intrinsic to worshipfulness.[14] Moreover, the people charged with overseeing prayer-book revisions were not the chaplains but scholars who had very different concerns on their minds; they simply renewed, in modern and largely Anglo-Catholic dress, the same evangelical/ traditionalist arguments that had afflicted work on the prayer book since the days of Cranmer and Knox. As things turned out, neither the Revised Version of the Bible, nor any of the early twentieth-century prayer books, nor even the Revised Standard Version of 1952, would tamper with the "thees and thous." That kind of linguistic change, though hoped for since the Great War and even before, would not occur until the 1960s—as we shall see.

The project of prayer-book revision also had to be conceived within the context of an international Anglicanism. English, Canadian, and American scholars worked on the same issues, using the same historical texts, and they shared their thoughts with one another. The process was smoother for the nonestablished churches, or should have been: the Anglicans of Canada issued a new *Book of Common Prayer* in 1922, but it took the Episcopalians a few years longer. No major changes were contemplated by the American revisers, but that seems simply to have made minor ones loom large. For instance, a great deal of energy was expended in trying to decide where—not whether, but where—to put a prayer, the so-called Prayer of Humble Access, in the Communion rite.[15] In general, the 1928 American revision slightly moderates the earlier books' emphasis on human sinfulness, especially by providing options for less penitential openings to Morning and Evening Prayer. It also makes a subtle but significant, and perhaps rather forward-looking, alteration to the rite for Holy Matrimony. In all previous books the husband had pledged "to love and to cherish" his wife—that beautiful addition of Cranmer's to the medieval rite—while she had pledged "to love, cherish, and to obey."

The 1928 American book eliminates "to obey" and in so doing makes the pledges of husband and wife almost identical, the only remaining difference being that the husband concludes by saying "and thereto I plight thee my troth," while the wife replies, "and thereto I give thee my troth"—as it had been since 1549.

Some complained that these changes marked a liberalizing of the church's teaching, but the complaints were not very loud. Across the Atlantic strife was more open, largely because of the long-established party divisions in the Church of England. So little were the various parties able to collaborate that each was allowed to develop its own prayer book, with the idea that once that work was complete the necessary horse trading could begin in earnest. This could not be construed as an indicator of hopefulness. One vigorously Anglo-Catholic group produced what came to be called the Green Book; another, somewhat more centrist, group of the same persuasion issued the Orange Book; and from a lower-church and relatively liberal group emerged the Grey Book. No book emerged from the evangelical camp because they proclaimed themselves largely satisfied with the existing one—as did Cambridge University in an official statement. One bishop presented to his fellow bishops a petition denouncing revision with the possibly unbelievable number of more than 300,000 signatures. Nevertheless, the English House of Bishops devoted much of the years 1925 to 1927 striving to transform the three colored books into a single one the country could accept.

The American revision, whose process of development was in comparison simplicity itself, came out in 1928, but the work of the Episcopalians' English colleagues would never see the light of day—at least, not formally. For once more the specter of establishment returned to haunt the Church of England; ancient polemics came back to life, old enmities found renewed vigor. The strongest-minded parties were unalterably opposed to the project: the highest Anglo-Catholics repudiated a book that retained so much of what some of them called the "pestilence" of Protestantism, while the most ardent evangelicals refused to tolerate one that not only retained its old flirtations with popery but also made room for new ones. The resisters were perhaps not large in number but they were loud of voice and could draw on the large sectors of the populace who were for whatever reason resistant to change; moreover, some of them held seats in Parliament. After the new book was endorsed by fairly large but not wholly comfortable majorities in the necessary church bodies and in the House of Lords, the bill authorizing its use failed in the House of Commons, by a vote of 238 to 205, in December of 1927.

One angry churchman commented, "In a single hectic night the House of Commons had apparently destroyed the work of more than twenty years."[16] Such bitterness was perhaps justified, but there had been, as we have seen, a good deal of writing on the political wall for those inclined to read it. Perhaps more decisive than the hostility of the evangelical and Anglo-Catholic extremes was the mild indifference of Archbishop Randall Davidson, who had simply never believed the long revision process to be a good use of the church's time. Nevertheless, the leading advocates for the revision convinced themselves that if they made a few minor alterations in a Protestant direction—for instance, making mandatory the Prayers for the Sovereign that Anglo-Catholic opponents of Establishment so disliked—and did a better job of educating the MPs, they could get the bill reintroduced and passed. Reintroduced it was; pass it did not. In June of 1928 it failed again in a fuller House of Commons, this time 266 to 220.

And that is why, as I write these words in 2012, the only official *Book of Common Prayer* of the Church of England is a very slightly altered version of the one introduced in 1662.

📖

The entire controversy about revisions to the English prayer book testifies to a single overwhelming fact: the success of Anglo-Catholicism in resetting the liturgical playing field in the Anglican world. In the 1920s, few argued for a revision of the prayer book in a more Protestant direction, and the few who did went unheard. Evangelicals were generally happy to stand pat with the 1662 book, though their ancestors would have leaped at the opportunity to remove every last vestige of popery. As John Betjeman points out, the average mid-twentieth-century evangelical vicar offered Communion far more frequently than would have been imaginable in Jane Austen's era, and wore vestments and furnished his Communion table in ways that in 1840 would simply have stunk of Rome—but found himself nevertheless looked upon by the nearby Anglo-Catholic parish as hopelessly low church.[17]

By 1928 Morning and Evening Prayer had shrunk in significance across the Anglican world. In many thousands of parishes in England and elsewhere Morning Prayer remained the standard Sunday morning service, but with each year that passed after 1840 Holy Communion gained ground, as a direct result of the dynamism of the Anglo-Catholic movement and its success in linking its focus on the Eucharist with the origins of the prayer book itself. Moreover, it had become clear throughout the Anglican Communion—indeed, throughout much of the world—that church was no longer going to be a daily experience for many Christians. If people were going to attend church weekly, at most, then it made sense for that experience to be a distinctive and powerful one, ceremonially significant and centered on the reception of the "spiritual food and drink" of the bread and wine. For these reasons, the attention of all the various prayer book revisers in the 1920s focused on the Eucharistic rite.

I noted in chapter 2 the view, first clearly articulated by Gregory Dix in 1945 and now dominant among scholars, that the Communion rite of 1552 is an ideal articulation of the Zwinglian belief that what happens in Communion is merely memorial: "This do in remembrance of me," Jesus said, and Communion is meant simply to remind us of what he did on our behalf. Dix argues that while the 1549 language allowed for, and perhaps even encouraged, interpretations of the rite that veered far closer to the traditional Catholic view, 1552 put those interpretations out of court. But when Elizabeth came to the throne, she clearly sympathized with traditionalist views, and the author of the definitive articulation of the Elizabethan settlement, Richard Hooker, plainly affirms that Christ is truly present in the Eucharistic elements:

> For we take not baptism nor the eucharist for bare *resemblances* or memorials of things absent, neither for *naked signs* and testimonies assuring us of grace received before, but (as they are indeed and in verity) for means effectual whereby God when we take the sacraments delivereth into our hands that grace available unto eternal life, which grace the sacraments represent or signify.[18]

This is a straightforward denial of the Zwinglian stance, and yet Hooker lived under the authority of a prayer book (the 1559 version) almost identical to the 1552 book. Therefore, Dix argues, "a great part of

Anglican history is taken up with difficulties caused by the fact that the Anglican rite was framed with exquisite skill to express this doctrine [the Zwinglian memorial view] which the Anglican church [as exemplified by the great Hooker] has always repudiated."[19]

Whether Dix is wholly right or not, he has certainly placed his finger precisely on the point of stress the revisers of the prayer book in the decade after the Great War were especially concerned to address. It seemed clear, to most of them anyway, that the prayer book spoke ambiguously, and perhaps inconsistently, to the increasingly widespread Eucharistic beliefs and practices of Anglicans. One example may stand in for many. In the 1549 book, the priest was instructed to give the bread to each communicant with these words: "The body of our Lord Jesus Christ which was given for thee, preserve thy body and soul unto everlasting life." (A similar sentence accompanied the administration of the wine.) For Bucer, Latimer, and others, perhaps including Cranmer himself, this sentence embodied the lamentable magical thinking of medieval Catholicism: it strongly suggests that transubstantiation has occurred, with the bread having *become* the Lord's Body, and that this transformed substance has the power to confer "everlasting life." So in 1552 this sentence was deleted and replaced by a Zwinglian one: "Take and eat this in remembrance that Christ died for thee, and feed on him in thy heart by faith, with thanksgiving." The object held between the priest's fingers is no longer "the body of our Lord" but merely an undefined "this," and all emphasis is placed on what happens, or ought to happen, inside the one receiving it: remembrance, faith, thanksgiving. When it came time to reinstitute the book in 1559, the church was therefore faced with a decision: Which sentence should be used? The leaders solved this puzzle neatly by stitching the two together and mandating both, a solution that was affirmed in 1662 and has ever since been cited as a shining example of Anglican inclusiveness.

But one person's inclusiveness is another's muddy-mindedness—especially when the inclusiveness in one part of the liturgy is accompanied by rubrics elsewhere that would seem to exclude the same views. For example, the 1549 rubrics are somewhat vague about the kind of bread to be used for Communion, but all of the later books contain this admonition: "And to take away all occasion of dissension, and superstition, which any Person hath or might have concerning the Bread and the Wine, it shall suffice that the Bread be such as is usual to be eaten; but the best and purest Wheat Bread that conveniently may be gotten." The point here is to forbid wafers, which had come into use in the Middle Ages in order to avoid the blasphemy of allowing crumbs of the Lord's Body to fall to the ground, there to be trampled or eaten by animals. The mandating of ordinary wheat bread is meant to exclude the very belief in transubstantiation that seems to be allowed, at least, by the sentence "The body of our Lord Jesus Christ which was given for thee, preserve thy body and soul unto everlasting life." The 1662 *Book of Common Prayer* was full of such inconsistencies and jury-rigged accommodations, and one of the chief tasks of revision, in the eyes of many revisers, was to clarify all such matters, especially those that had led to prosecutions in the later Victorian era. Nothing marked an Anglo-Catholic parish more clearly than the use of Communion wafers, in direct defiance of the rubric, but in obedient acknowledgment (or so the priest would say) of the more generous implications of the Communion rite's actual words.

In such contentious circumstances, the prayer book's revisers may perhaps be forgiven for failing to give attention to the "thees and thous." But even if so, their work was little respected. Not only was it repudiated by Parliament, but also subsequent episcopal approval for the revised rites to be used experimentally—in what amounted to defiance of Parliament, though never acknowledged as such—got no real traction. Anglicans preferred the old book, in part because the new one was not sufficiently different from its predecessors to have any strong virtues to recommend it. Perhaps the fairest verdict to make on the early twentieth-century revisions of the *Book of Common Prayer*, in England and elsewhere, is simply that the time was not ripe for them. It was only later that momentum began to develop, around the world and among Roman Catholics as well as various Protestant bodies, for serious reconsideration of the Christian liturgies. What we now know as the Liturgical Movement achieved its first real influence in the 1930s, and out of that movement emerged a book—a book by an Anglican—that would have a massive influence on liturgical revision throughout the world. And one of the chief ways this Anglican's book established its provocative stance toward Eucharistic prayer was by rejecting, almost tout court, the work of Thomas Cranmer.

📖

The book is called *The Shape of the Liturgy*, and it was written during World War II by an Anglican Benedictine monk whom we have already encountered: Gregory Dix. Six hundred of the book's 750 pages say nothing about Anglicanism, instead tracing the developments of the Eucharistic liturgy from the earliest known records up to the late Middle Ages, and Dix repeatedly insists that he only added a chapter on the development of Anglican liturgy because several of his fellow Anglicans insisted that he do so. Of "the work of Archbishop Cranmer" he insists that "in the whole story it is no more than an incident, and that of no central interest to the subject of liturgy as a whole."[20] But few who have read the whole book can take this demurral seriously. It is impossible not to think that the book was written precisely in order to dethrone Cranmer, to repudiate his work, and to exhort Anglicans to set their liturgy on firmer and better footing. Dix, who eagerly sought reunion with Rome, knew what *he* thought that firmer footing should be, but many who read his book did not share his tendencies and yet came away with a sense that the whole long process of prayer-book revision had been fundamentally misconceived, and needed to be reconceived along Dixian lines.

Although illustrated by a great mass of historical detail, Dix's core argument is relatively simple. He begins with St. Paul's words in 1 Corinthians 11: "The Lord Jesus the same night in which he was betrayed took bread: And when he had given thanks, he brake it, and said, Take, eat: this is my body, which is broken for you: this do in remembrance of me. After the same manner also he took the cup, when he had supped, saying, this cup is the new testament in my blood: this do ye, as oft as ye drink it, in remembrance of me." From this passage Dix infers a simple four-stage "shape" of Eucharistic prayer: *taking* the bread or wine, *praying* over it, *breaking* it, and *giving* it to his disciples. Or, in the terms of liturgical structure, the *offertory*, the *invocation*, the *fraction*, and the *communion* proper. "The underlying structure is always the same because the essential action is always the same, and this standard structure or Shape alone embodies and expresses the full and complete eucharistic action for all churches and all races and all times." Moreover, "wherever the standard structure of the rite has been broken up or notably altered, there it will be found that some part of the primitive fulness of the meaning of the eucharist has been lost," and this loss will inevitably damage "the christian *living* of those whose christianity has been thus impoverished."[21] It is this shape and only this shape that is essential to healthy and proper Eucharistic prayer. The search for some original, or at least very ancient, form of *words* has been a scholarly wild-goose chase; though the words of any Eucharistic prayer should conform to, and illustrate, the four-fold shape, Dix doubts that any given early church community even *had* one fixed set of words in which to perform this rite.

The implications of this argument for thought about the prayer book proved enormous. Until Dix, the standard Anglo-Catholic view had gone something like this: Cranmer's 1549 Eucharistic rite struck a balance between Catholic tradition and necessary reform, whereas the 1552 book had veered too strongly in the Reformed or Zwinglian direction. The Ornaments Rubric, with its reference to "the Second Year of the Reign of King Edward the Sixth," that is, 1549, implicitly acknowledged the practices of that year, and not 1552, as the standard to which Anglicans should refer themselves. Therefore any appropriate revision of the prayer book should take the 1549 Communion rite as its chief reference point, though, since Cranmer himself was seeking to anchor his liturgy in the most ancient texts available, we who have more ancient witnesses to draw upon than Cranmer could have dreamed of may rightly honor his wishes by using those ancient rites in our revision.

Dix effectively shattered this whole structure of thought, and did so with multiple blows. First, as already noted, he rendered the search for a single ancient authoritative set of words nugatory. Second, he argued that the 1549 rite had deviated grossly from the fourfold Shape and was therefore liturgically heretical. And this was not its only sin; by trying to retain as much of Catholic tradition as possible while importing Reformation ideas, Cranmer ended up with little more than "a disordered attempt at a Catholic rite"—an incoherent liturgical mishmash. By contrast, the Communion rite of 1552 is "the masterpiece of an artist," "a superb piece of literature," and, most important, "the only effective attempt ever made to give liturgical expression to the doctrine of 'justification by faith alone.'"[22] But this is Dix speaking as a connoisseur of liturgical art, not as a theologian; theologically, he deplores the 1552 rite, because he rejects its governing ideas, especially the Zwinglian view of the Communion service as a purely memorial one.

So by the time Dix gets finished with Cranmer, virtually nothing remains of the archbishop's supposed achievement. Dix argues that liturgical renewal cannot build on the foundation of the 1549 rite, because it neglects the classic fourfold Shape and in addition is intellectually and theologically incoherent; nor can such renewal base itself on the 1552 rite, because it rejects Catholic tradition altogether, in ways the Anglican world has never wanted to face. Before Dix, Anglo-Catholics had believed that they possessed a rich Cranmerian inheritance on which they could draw; after Dix, this belief became far more difficult to sustain, and many abandoned it altogether.

Dix believed that any Anglicans who shared the Zwinglian understanding of the Communion and the Reformation commitment to justification by faith alone could be perfectly happy with the 1552 rite and its direct successor, the very minor revision of 1662. No wonder, then, that in the 1920s the evangelical party professed itself content with the Restoration book and didn't trouble itself to come up with a revision. But those of a higher-church persuasion needed to look elsewhere. Dix thought it obvious that that "elsewhere" was Rome, but many who accepted his demolition of Cranmer did not draw that conclusion. Rather, they focused on Dix's insistence that the Shape is what matters and the specific words of the prayer secondary and derivative. For these people, Dix's argument was liberating; rather than having to defer always to Cranmer, they could pursue serious liturgical innovation, providing always that they adhered to the Shape. This idea became tremendously influential throughout the worldwide Liturgical Movement, and even among Roman Catholics as the Second Vatican Council drew near. But Dix's argument bore its first fruits not in England, or America, or Rome, but rather in southern India. And it was there that a great shift of Anglican energies—in liturgy and in almost all other aspects of the Christian life—really began.

Liturgical innovation had, in fact, already begun in the southern hemisphere: revised Eucharistic rites had been introduced in Zanzibar in 1918, and in Rhodesia soon afterward.[23] Few in the North noticed. But when the Church of South India produced new rites in the 1950s, the whole liturgical world noticed. And this was in part because their work was based so strongly on Dix's arguments.

The Church of South India (CSI) was formed in 1947, just months after Indian independence, to unite Anglicans in the southern part of that country and in Ceylon (as it was then known) with various Protestant bodies: Methodists, Congregationalists, and Presbyterians.[24] It was an exercise in Christian ecumenism and consequently needed forms of worship that could be adapted to varying circumstances, and, indeed, that could be ignored by those congregations who preferred more spontaneous worship. Moreover, the rites needed to be in languages other than English—they first appeared in Tamil, Telegu, Malayalam, and Kannada—and suited for congregations with widely varying degrees of literacy. The more that could be drawn from long-standing Indian Christian traditions, especially the Orthodox Liturgy of St. James, the better. (There seems to have been no thought of creating a prayer book per se, only a series of necessary rites, beginning with Holy Communion, but by 1963 the liturgical work was sufficiently complete that it could be collected in a *Book of Common Worship*.)

Most of the people charged with making these liturgies were English, but the most important leaders of the Church of South India sought what would later be called full *inculturation*: encouraging in any given culture the emergence of indigenous forms of Christianity. Leslie Brown, who headed the CSI's Liturgy Commission, later became Archbishop of Uganda but returned to his native England for the specific purpose of allowing Ugandans to assume leadership over their own church. The greatest leader of the CSI, and possibly the greatest bishop-theologian of the twentieth century, Lesslie Newbigin, wrote a Christian primer largely in Tamil, and after his retirement and return to England commented that the work of the missionary was just this: "there must be a congregation furnished with the Bible, the sacraments, and the apostolic ministry. When these conditions are fulfilled, the missionary has done her job. The young church is then free to learn, as it goes and grows, how to embody the gospel in its own culture."[25] Armed with this model of cultural empowerment, the old liturgies of the Indian church, and the principles of Gregory Dix, the liturgists of the Church of South India embarked on the creation of a Communion rite.[26]

Those who have worshipped in an Episcopal church in the United States, and in many other Anglican churches around the world, will find certain features common to the rite of Holy Communion. There will be four Scripture readings, one usually taken from an Old Testament book other than the Psalms, one from the Psalms (said or sung), one from a New Testament book other than the Gospels, and one from a Gospel. Just before the Communion prayer the Peace is exchanged: "The peace of the Lord be always with you," "And also with you" or "And with your spirit." Laypersons bring the bread and wine to the table, where the priest receives it. The Eucharistic prayer is called the Great Thanksgiving. The priest faces the people as he or she says this prayer. Most of these practices emerge from the teaching of Dix, and all of them find their first modern embodiment in the rites of the Church of South India.

By the time the Lambeth Conference—the once-a-decade meeting of bishops from the worldwide Anglican Communion—met in 1958, the CSI liturgy had been in use for several years, and pamphlets containing its Eucharistic rite had circulated around the world. Those attending Lambeth were also well aware of the energies of the Liturgical Movement within the Roman Catholic Church, energies that would find their outlet when the Second Vatican Council was convened four years later. They could see that further revision of the prayer book was inevitable, but were unsure quite what to do about it; they therefore managed only to pass a series of vague and innocuous resolutions that amounted to little more than an acknowledgment that the ground was moving under their feet.[27]

Soon it was moving more dramatically. In 1964 Leslie Brown, now Archbishop of Uganda, published a major project that grew out of the South India work, *A Liturgy for Africa*. This proved to be a landmark work in its own way, not as liturgically innovative as the CSI Eucharistic rite, but establishing the need for African churches not just to translate the 1662 *Book of Common Prayer*—something that had been done for dozens of African languages from the late nineteenth through the early twentieth centuries—but to develop their own culturally appropriate forms of common worship. This impulse would soon spread throughout the Anglican world.

But the *Liturgy for Africa* was at the time scarcely noticed because a few months earlier, in December of 1963, the first major document of the Second Vatican Council had been issued: the *Constitution on the Sacred Liturgy*. This document is most famous for its authorization of masses in vernacular languages, which ended the four-hundred-year dominance of the Latin Tridentine rite, but in the Anglican world, what mattered more was the creation of *multiple* rites for the Mass—not just the familiar and venerable Roman Canon, but a series of three alternate Eucharistic prayers, based on ancient sources, to be used within any given parish. If even Rome no longer felt it necessary to have "but one use," why should Anglicans insist on the point? Pope Paul VI did not authorize the new Mass and its alternative Eucharistic prayers until 1968, but their presence had been known for some time, and throughout the Anglican world a thousand liturgical flowers bloomed. Although Morning and Evening Prayer got some attention, along with the baptismal liturgy, these were mainly revisions of or alternatives to the Communion rite, which were quickly authorized for experimental use and, especially in America, quickly adopted in many parishes.

It soon became clear that the next American *Book of Common Prayer*, to be released in 1979, would follow the Roman model by offering multiple versions of the same rites. In 1974 the Church of England authorized the creation of an Alternative Service Book (ASB)—so called because as long as the *Book of Common Prayer* itself was not tampered with, Parliament need not become entangled in the deliberations. The ASB that emerged a few years later followed the same ramifying and multiplying pattern. The book Cranmer created, so carefully modified over the next century, so minutely adjusted in the many years that succeeded, was now being urged, not always gently, to the sidelines of Anglican liturgical life.

FIGURE 7. The Standard Book of the 1928 American prayer book, designed by Daniel Berkeley Updike and printed by the Merrymount Press, is a masterpiece of American bookmaking.

Photograph courtesy of the Francis Donaldson Library at Nashotah House Theological Seminary.

Many Books for Many Countries

CHAPTER 7

Among those who treasured the old prayer book, the poet W. H. Auden offered a typical response. When his parish in Greenwich Village, St. Mark's Church in-the-Bowery, tried out the new rites in the late 1960s, Auden wrote a letter to the rector that began, "Dear Father Allen: Have you gone stark raving mad?"

The poet went on, in only slightly less vivid language, to make arguments many traditionalists would repeat in the coming years, though rarely with Auden's incisiveness.

> Our Church has had the singular good-fortune
> of having its Prayer-Book composed and its
> Bible translated at exactly the right time, ie, late
> enough for the language to be intelligible to any
> english-speaking person in this century (any
> child of six can be taught what "the quick and
> the dead" means) and early enough, ie, when
> people still had an instinctive feeling for the for-

mal and the ceremonious which is essential in liturgical language.

This feeling has been, alas, as we all know, almost totally lost. (To identify the ceremonious with "the undemocratic" is sheer contemporary cant.) The poor Roman Catholics, obliged to start from scratch, have produced an English Mass which is a cacophonous monstrosity . . . But why should we imitate them?

I implore you by the bowels of Christ to stick to Cranmer and King James. Preaching, of course, is another matter: there the language must be contemporary. But one of the great functions of the liturgy is to keep us in touch with the past and the dead.[1]

In their more sober and, perhaps, honest moments, though, even the most impassioned advocates for the old prayer book had to concede that it had problems. There were the liturgical ones on which Dix had shone so pitiless a light, but also issues stemming from the inclusion of so much Scripture in the book—Scripture in translations that now could be seen to be full of errors.

Most of the biblical passages in the prayer book were taken from the King James version, except for the Psalms: these continued to be in the Miles Coverdale version of 1535. During the debates just after the Restoration, some had advocated for the King James versions to replace Coverdale, but his words were too beloved, at least in the context of public worship. It was good to *read* "The Lord is my shepherd; I shall not want," but better, it seems, to *chant* "The Lord is my shepherd; therefore can I lack nothing." However, it became increasingly clear that, to put it bluntly, Coverdale had not known Hebrew very well. As C. S. Lewis put it, "Even of the old translators he is by no means the most accurate; and of course a sound modern scholar has more Hebrew in his little finger than poor Coverdale had in his whole body."[2] As a reward, or perhaps a punishment, for this comment, Lewis was asked in the very same year to serve on the Church of England's newly created Commission to Revise the Psalter. He was joined on this committee by, among others, T. S. Eliot.

Three years later Lewis had come to see that by conceding the errors and emphasizing the beauty in Coverdale he had perhaps erred. In a letter to a friend in 1961 he noted as "absurd" "what I'm fighting against on the Commission for revising the Coverdale Psalter—I mean, the impulse to retain what we know to be mere howlers because they are 'so beautiful.'"[3] In the end, he and Eliot settled on the view that, while the Psalter to be included in the prayer book had to be revised, "Coverdale's Psalter should continue to be available and, if possible, to be widely known."[4] The two literary lions did not specify how this was to be achieved.

As the pace of prayer-book revision and liturgical innovation accelerated throughout the last decades of the twentieth century, groups began to form in the Anglo-American world to resist this change. Largely in response to the American book of 1979, the *Alternative Service Book* in England, and the *Book of Alternative Services* in Canada—all of which emerged at roughly the same time, in keeping with the international character of Anglican liturgical work that had been established in the 1920s—there arose in each country a Prayer Book Society. The Canadian group says that it "upholds the maintenance of the Prayer Book as the official standard of doctrine and worship in the Anglican Church of Canada (while supporting a modest amount of flexibility as may be sensible and locally appropriate)." The American one "claims that the Constitution of the Episcopal Church gives to Rectors and parishes, as well as to individual Episcopalians, the right to use the last genuine Book of Common Prayer in America: the 1928 BCP." The English group wishes to "restore the respect" for the 1662 book "which was in danger of being lost. . . . The aim of the Society is still to ensure that the Book of Common Prayer is still used and honoured, available for worship wherever it is desired."[5]

What do these supporters of the older books find to deplore in the new ones? A great deal, though their discomforts come in varying forms and varying degrees of intensity. They feel the loss of familiar words and phrases, and they struggle to adjust when asked to say, in response to the priest's "The Lord be with you," "And also with you" instead of the time-honored "And with thy spirit." Addressing the priest, and still more God Himself, as "you" feels uncomfortably casual (in spite of the fact that "thee" and "thou" were once the pronouns of intimacy, not formality). Further, they feel that many of the linguistic changes amount to doctrinal changes as well. For instance, here is the General Confession in the 1662 book's rite for Holy Communion, retained in the 1928 American book:

> Almighty God, Father of our Lord Jesus Christ, Maker of all things, judge of all men; We acknowledge and bewail our manifold sins and wickedness, Which we, from time to time, most grievously have committed, By thought, word, and deed, Against thy Divine Majesty, Provoking most justly thy wrath and indignation against us. We do earnestly repent, And are heartily sorry for these our misdoings; The remembrance of them is grievous unto us; The burden of them is intolerable. Have mercy upon us, Have mercy upon us, most merciful Father; For thy Son our Lord Jesus Christ's sake, Forgive us all that is past; And grant that we may ever hereafter Serve and please thee In newness of life, To the honour and glory of thy Name; Through Jesus Christ our Lord. Amen.[6]

That prayer remains as an option in what the 1979 American *Book of Common Prayer* calls "Rite I," its traditional-language rite, but in Rite II, the modern-language liturgy that most parishes now use, it is replaced by this:

> Most merciful God, we confess that we have sinned against you in thought, word, and deed, by what we have done, and by what we have left undone. We have not loved you with our whole heart; we have not loved our neighbors as ourselves. We are truly sorry and we humbly repent. For the sake of your Son Jesus Christ, have mercy on us and forgive us; that we may delight in your will, and walk in your ways, to the glory of your Name. *Amen*.[7]

This is certainly penitent, but in the eyes of many traditionalists only moderately so. "We have not loved you with our whole heart" could be read as "We're not perfect, but we're not so bad," a construal that can scarcely be placed on "We acknowledge and bewail our manifold sins and wickedness." To be "truly sorry" is one thing; to be "heartily sorry for these our misdoings" and to go on to say that "the remembrance of them is grievous unto us; The burden of them is intolerable"—that, traditionalists argue, is something else altogether.

Now, a strong and thoroughly orthodox justification can be given for these changes. Marion Hatchett, for instance, has pointed out that "in this form we confess not only our sins of commission but also those of omission and our lack of love for God and neighbor. Not only do we ask that we may walk in God's ways, but also that we may delight in His will."[8] For Hatchett, the new Confession asks *more* from us than the old one. Others argue rather that the moderated language of the new Confession is better suited to the people of God, who come to the table as baptized Christians, having in the first part of the service already heard the Word of God, affirmed it, and exchanged the Peace with one another. On *this* account overwhelmingly penitential language is simply not appropriate; it is not a fast to which we trudge in sackcloth and ashes, but the "Eucharistic feast" to which we should come joyfully. But neither sort of defense convinces the traditionalists, who also note that the Prayer of Humble Access— whose relocation in the 1928 book had prompted so much controversy—is excised from the new Rite II altogether.

Other aspects of the new book appear to traditionalists as mere silliness, especially Rite II's Eucharistic Prayer C, sometimes known in either affection or contempt as the "Star Wars prayer": "At your command all things came to be; the vast expanse of interstellar space, galaxies, suns, the planets in their courses, and this fragile earth, our island home." To those accustomed to Cranmer's sober cadences, no adherence to Dix's apostolic fourfold pattern can possibly defend *this*. (It is my impression that few defend this prayer nowadays, since its roots in the Age of Aquarius are rather too evident. But it might be worth noting that of the four Eucharistic prayers in

Rite II this one places the greatest emphasis on the Fall, and its phrase "the planets in their courses" is a surprising echo of the King James version's rendering of Judges 5:20, from the Song of Deborah: "The stars in their courses fought against Sisera.")

To such accusations of crimes against language, against doctrine, against liturgical decorum, defenders of the new rites often point out that all such innovations are optional; perhaps one's priest can be convinced to use one of the other Eucharistic prayers, or to offer a Rite I service (in England called a "1662 service" or simply a "Prayer Book service") from time to time, in Lent perhaps, or, more likely, as an early morning option for elderly parishioners who, as Ecclesiastes reminds us, "rise up at the voice of the bird." But many traditionalists reply that the very existence of such options, of such a buffet, is the greatest offense of all. For we no longer have Cranmer's insistence on "one use" within a given parish, much less throughout the land. There is no longer anything truly *common* about our prayers, and to many traditionalists, and even to quite a few Anglicans who are not especially traditional in their doctrinal or linguistic preferences, this is the harshest blow and the greatest loss.

But it is impossible to conceive of any circumstances that might lead to a consolidation of the forms of Anglican worship. Defenders of liturgical alternatives rightly note that Anglicans, even within a given country, are now unprecedentedly diverse in their cultural backgrounds and religious experiences and expectations. It is certain that much liturgical development, within Anglicanism and within the Roman orbit as well, has been driven by the earnest desire to create a body of public prayer that can collectively be all things to all people. But it is also certain that Newman was right when he said that "a taste for criticism grows upon the mind," and that the "temper of innovation," once given its head, cannot subsequently be restrained. And in a digital age there are fewer restraints upon innovation than ever.

In previous generations the ability to put forth (if not to create) new liturgies was always constrained by the limitations of the central technology: the codex book. The prayers offered for the people's use had to fit between two covers. All versions of the *Book of Common Prayer* through the American book of 1928 contained the New Testament readings (Epistle and Gospel alike) appointed for each Sunday, but these were excised from the 1979 American book in order to make room for the new options: two versions of Morning Prayer, two versions of Evening Prayer, a new "Order of Worship for the evening," a Rite I Eucharist with two alternative Eucharistic prayers, a Rite II Eucharist with four alternative Eucharistic prayers, various choices of anthems and collects within each of these rites, and so on and so on. The result is nearly a thousand pages long: a book right at the edge of unwieldiness, even with modern printing technologies—including, necessarily, very thin paper.

Yet liturgical innovation has not ceased; in fact, it has only increased its momentum, with the inestimable aid of the Internet as a means of dissemination. In this light consider the successor to the *Alternative Service Book* in the Church of England, the project known as Common Worship. Although the rites produced via Common Worship have appeared in a number of different books—including *Common Worship: Services and Prayers for the Church of England*, *Common Worship: The President's Edition*, *Common Worship: Pastoral Services*, *Common Worship: Christian Initiation*, *Common Worship: Daily Prayer*, *Common Worship: Collects and Post Communions*, and *New Patterns for Worship*—the project exists in its fullness only online. Its website describes its purpose: "Common Worship is not just another prayer book, but a series of volumes which aims to provide a wide variety of prayers and liturgical resources for use within a common framework and common structures. This allows individual churches to tailor services to their own setting and culture and the needs of their particular congregations."[9] Perusing these resources, one discovers, within the rites for Holy Communion, an Order One, with eight different Eucharistic prayers, and an Order Two in both traditional and contemporary language. The page for Morning and Evening Prayer contains among its options "The Acclamation of Christ at the Dawning of the Day," "The Blessing of the Light," "Morning and Evening Prayer in Ordinary Time," "Morning and Evening Prayer in Seasonal Time," "Thanksgivings for Use at Morning and Evening Prayer," "Prayers for the Unity of the Church," "Prayers at the Foot of the Cross," "A Commemoration of the Resurrection," and the "Vigil Office." The website also contains the *Book of Common Prayer*, in my (codex) copy of which Morning and Evening Prayer comprise twenty-five pages. The equivalent volume in the new series, *Common Worship: Daily Prayer*, is 903 pages long. It also prints the Lord's Prayer and the Apostles' Creed on the back endpapers and features six differently colored ribbons to help users keep track of what they are doing when they use it to pray.[10]

The Common Worship approach to liturgy is sometimes called *modular*; I have heard its disparagers call it "liturgical Legos." Although that papalist Anglo-Catholic Gregory Dix would likely swoon at much of the work produced by recent liturgists, they are following in his footsteps by trumping *language* with *structure*. The core idea is to give pastors the ability to choose from among many options the ones that best fit their own theological and spiritual commitments, the needs of the local parish, and the varying emphases of the seasons of the church year. There are prayers on the Common Worship site to suit every tendency within the big tent of Anglicanism and every mood of the Christian life, and much of what is on offer there represents brilliant liturgical scholarship and the adaptation of ancient and noble rites to contemporary contexts. By contrast, the dangers of the modular approach are incoherence within a given service, if mismatched parts are chosen, and a bewildering instability for the congregation, who, if they have an experimental or seasonally sensitive or just plain fidgety pastor, will never spend enough time in any given rite to memorize it—to learn well even a part of it. (Those who feel that "rote learning" should be discouraged welcome this.)

But whatever one thinks about the pastoral consequences of the modular approach, it must be said that if earlier bursts of liturgical activity had eliminated the "common" from Anglican prayer life, modularity removes the "book." Few churches could afford copies of the many different books listed above for distribution to the pews, and even if the expense could be spared, the logistical challenge of switching out books from season to season and service to service would be impossible to meet. In practice, the prayers from Common Worship are selected, copied from the website, and pasted into documents for printing in pamphlets or display on screens. Although ordinary parishioners are free to buy their own copies of the various Common Worship books, it is not clear why many of them would want to do so.

There has never been unanimity in Anglican worship, but for a long time—the time when Morning Prayer reigned as the dominant liturgy—broad agreement prevailed. One could enter almost any Anglican church in the world and experience the same words, the same order. The first resistance to such unanimity came from the Scots ("Will ye say the Mass in my lug?") who preferred their "wee bookies" to any mandate emerging from Canterbury. Then came a full-fledged and different book, in the new country of the United States; then a century of minor adjustments in various corners of the empire and the ex-empire; then the translation of the *Book of Common Prayer* into African and Asian languages. Cranmer's book, as edited by his successors, proved to be enormously adaptable—but not infinitely so.

Stewart Brand has written a book called *How Buildings Learn*,[11] and there is a sense in which books learn too: the best of them shape themselves to the contours of different cultural environments. Consider the wildly variable uses to which the Bible has been put, or the redeployment of Sophocles's *Antigone* against multiple political tyrannies, or the wonderfully endless reinterpretation of the Shakespearean oeuvre. But a religious book is limited in its ability to learn because it is concerned to *teach*; and a prayer book especially wants its teaching to be enacted, not just to be absorbed. It cannot live unless we say its words in our voices. It can learn with us, but only if we consent to learn from it. There are relatively few, now, who give that consent to the *Book of Common Prayer*. Cranmer's book, and its direct successors, will always be acknowledged as historical documents of the first order, and masterpieces of English prose, but this is not what they want or mean to be. Their goal—now as in 1549—is to be living words in the mouths of those who have a living faith.

The Prayer Book and Its Printers

In the beginning, not just anyone could print the *Book of Common Prayer*. The Crown had to grant a license. The only licensed printers of the first prayer book were Londoners, Richard Grafton and Edward Whitchurch—two distinct printing businesses, but the men had once been partners, and in those days had printed Matthew's Bible in 1537 and Coverdale's in 1538. This placed them squarely on the side of the Reformers, and indeed the actual printing of those books had to be done on Continental presses. Now, with Reformers in the ascendent, they reaped the rewards of their faithfulness to the evangelical cause.[1]

The first *Book of Common Prayer* to appear, on March 7, 1549, came from Whitchurch. (Interestingly, he worked out of the Fleet Street shop that once belonged to Wynken de Worde, the second great printer in England after William Caxton.) He and Grafton lost their place under Mary, of course, and never got it back: the right to print prayer books passed to others in Elizabeth's reign. Eventually the license went to the Barker family, who also printed the Authorized, or King James, version of the Bible. The Barker family held the license until 1709, when it was purchased by a man named John Baskett.

Many of the first prayer books were of folio size, intended for public display. In many parishes such a copy would have been the only local one. However, and perhaps surprisingly, a good many smaller prayer books survive from the Tudor era, including some so tiny as to be unreadable. These would presumably have been kept as talismans, to indicate one's loyalties or to ward off evil. In them we see books assuming the kind of symbolic power more typically associated with the appurtenances of Catholicism: crucifixes, rosary beads, consecrated bread. Right from the start the books could be bought bound or unbound, in the latter case so that the owner could have his or her own binding made, or so the prayer book could be bound together with a copy of the Bible—later, with metrical Psalters and then hymnals.

(In the early stages of writing this book I had the privilege of visiting Lambeth Palace, where I met with the then Archbishop of Canterbury, Rowan Williams. Next to the chair in which he did much of his reading was a very large eighteenth-century book, covered in worn leather and featuring two buckles to hold its boards closed. It was clear from the way the archbishop held this book, passing his fingers delicately over the pages, that it was dear to him. It held, bound together, the *Book of Common Prayer* and the Bible—in Welsh.)

The first prayer books were in blackletter type, the typeface seen in the earliest northern European books; virtually unreadable now, it was meant to imitate the handwriting of late medieval scribes. The shift to now-familiar roman type (pioneered in Venice by Nicolas Jenson around 1470) was gradual. The first *Book of Common Prayer* in roman type appeared in 1586, and the last blackletter one in 1707—far later than most would guess, but as we have seen, the prayer book had by then assumed a venerability that made some associate it with equally venerable kinds of type.

As we have also seen, Parliament banned the public use of the prayer book in 1641; using it became a penal offense in 1645. Some printers—many of them working on the Continent, as had printers of English Bibles a century earlier—printed new copies but dated them pre-1641 in order to disguise their own work and keep the prosecutors away. Also at this time prayer books started including lists of the original compilers and made a point of designating Cranmer as a martyr of the church.

The aforementioned John Baskett appears to have been a rapacious and litigious man who spent a great deal of time, energy, and money to increase his privileges to print prayer books and Bibles and to keep others from doing the same. He controlled Oxford's printing presses, then located, perhaps incongruously, in that early Christopher Wren masterpiece, the Sheldonian Theatre. Baskett seems not to have paid much attention to the quality of the work. In the early seventeenth century the Society for the Promoting of Christian Knowledge, a then-new Anglican missionary organization, began to scrutinize prayer books he had printed and report on their ever-proliferating errors. When he died in 1742 his work passed to his son Mark, who seems to have taken still less care. A pamphlet printed in Oxford in 1764, in the midst of a heated dispute about licensing that involved Baskett and rival printers, including one named Charles Eyre, contained this passage:

> Mr Basket lived upon a genteel Private Fortune and neither understood nor gave any Attention to the business of Printing. He left it therefore to the Care of his Servants who employed the Presses in printing a Great Number of small Prayer-books in 12mo for Foreign sale; so that what Mr Eyre alleged in his Memorial, was an indisputable Fact—"That most of the Chappels in Oxford were supply'd with Folio and Quarto Prayer Books from Cambridge". The Under Servants and Press Men were a set of Idle Drunken Men, and the House appeared more like an Ale House than a Printing Room.

Mark Baskett soon thereafter lost his license to print prayer books. At Cambridge the situation was quite different, as the pamphlet rightly reports, because that university's head printer from 1758 to 1775 was the great John Baskerville, best known today for the beautiful typeface that bears his name. (Although employed by Cambridge University, Baskerville lived and worked in Birmingham.) The typeface became famous through its employment in Bibles and prayer books, for which it is exceptionally well suited, but the printer himself was a convinced and open atheist.

It was in the nineteenth century that versions of the prayer book proliferated: small, large, ornamented, annotated. As noted earlier, some late nineteenth-century special, limited printings of the *Book of Common Prayer* were done by the usual "privileged" printers but with the added imprint of the Cunard cruise line or Boots the Chemist.

In the United States the *Book of Common Prayer* has never been copyrighted and can therefore be printed and distributed by anyone, but most editions—all of those churches use—are prefaced by a "certificate" from an authority of the Episcopal Church affirming that the book has been checked for accuracy against a copy of the "Standard Book." Such Standard Books were prepared for all versions of the American prayer book from 1793 through 1928, and are often very beautiful—none more so than the Standard Book prepared in 1928 by Daniel Berkeley Updike, the great printer of Merrymount Press in Boston. Set in Janson and elegantly designed, it is one of the shining achievements of American bookmaking. For reasons I have been unable to discover—but probably arising from the belief that digital typesetting makes reference standards for books obsolete—no Standard Book of the 1979 prayer book was ever made. But most American Episcopalians are familiar with its distinctive appearance, common across all versions, featuring the elegant Sabon typeface Jan Tschichold designed in the mid-1960s.

The *Common Worship* books in England are notable for their reliance on Gill Sans, perhaps the typographic masterpiece of the disturbed but brilliant Eric Gill, who created it in 1926. (It closely resembles the typeface Edward Johnston made for the London Underground, and indeed Gill worked with Johnston on that project for a time.) The major Common Worship books are magnificently designed by Omnific Design, the studio headed by Derek Birdsall. But many people today encounter those texts not in Omnific's lovely volumes with their masterful use of the various weights of Gill Sans but in whatever sans-serif font, probably Arial or Helvetica, their computer's browser uses to render HTML files. The less fortunate will find those texts simply copied and pasted into bulletins or projected on PowerPoint slides; the more fortunate will have someone at their church with the taste and the inclination to make the text as attractive as possible. But while the *Book of Common Prayer* lives on in so many ways, its association with the crafts of bookmaking and type design may have effectively come to an end.

ACKNOWLEDGMENTS

My first thanks go to Fred Appel, who graciously allowed me to write this book, which brought me much delight. I am also grateful to be working—for the third time—with the staff of Princeton University Press, who practice the crafts of bookmaking, from editing to designing to binding, with consistent excellence. Dawn Hall was a skilled and thorough copyeditor.

For assistance with the images included here, I owe a debt to David Sherwood and Ben Jeffries of Nashotah House in Wisconsin, and Sarah Werner of the Folger Shakespeare Library in Washington, DC.

I am grateful for the friends who walked with me through this process and offered advice, apt quotations, warm encouragement, and the occasional necessary puncturing of my various pretensions. Chief among these friends are Brett Foster, Richard Gibson, Wesley Hill, Tim Larsen, Dan Treier, Jay Wood, and two friends who are also priests and from whose lips I have frequently heard the words of the prayer book intoned: Chip Edgar and Martin Johnson. Let me also here give thanks for the people of All Souls' Anglican Church in Wheaton, Illinois, who have so often listened patiently as I have pontificated about some of the matters included here.

It's impossible for me to speak adequately of what my wife Teri means to me; I couldn't have written this book, and could scarcely do anything else, without her love and support. I hope I can speak also for her and say that we have known "the mutual society, help, and comfort, that the one ought to have of the other, both in prosperity and adversity."

I dedicate this book to my son Wesley, whom the words of the prayer book have accompanied from Baptism through Confirmation and now into adult life. He is the apple of my eye.

INTRODUCTION: The Archbishop in His Library

1. J. Cave-Browne, *Lambeth Palace and Its Associations* (Edinburgh and London: Blackwood, 1883), 367.

2. For a full assessment, see David Gordon Selwyn, *The Library of Thomas Cranmer* (Oxford: Oxford Bibliographical Society, 1996).

3. BCP 41–45.

4. See TC 328.

CHAPTER 1: One Book for One Country

1. E. W. Ives, "Henry VIII (1491–1547)," *Oxford Dictionary of National Biography* (Oxford: Oxford University Press, 2004); online edition, May 2009, http://www.oxforddnb.com/view/article/12955, accessed December 8, 2011. Further details in the following paragraphs are drawn largely from Ives's excellent brief biography.

2. I use the word "evangelical" in preference to "Protestant" for reasons Diarmaid MacCulloch noted: In the sixteenth century "Protestant" had a narrow meaning, confined to certain groups of German Christians,

whereas "evangelical" "was widely used and recognized at the time, and it also encapsulates what was most important to this collection of activists: the good news of the Gospel, in Latinized Greek, the *evangelium*." *The Reformation* (New York: Penguin, 2005), xx.

3. Throughout my account I will be treating Cranmer as the author of the first and second prayer books. A great deal of scholarly energy has been expended over the years in attempts to discover both the liturgical sources from which Cranmer worked and his likely collaborators. One of the best accounts of the former is G. J. Cuming, *The Godly Order: Texts and Studies Relating to the Book of Common Prayer* (London: Alcuin Club, 1983). The Brian Cummings edition of the prayer book I cite throughout this study is also highly informative about these sources. Diarmaid MacCulloch searches for possible collaborators in his biography of Cranmer but cannot discern any; see TC 416–17.

4. TC 360.

5. All of these articulations of the traditionalist position are quoted by Ramie Targoff in *Common Prayer: The Language of Public Devotion in Early Modern England* (Chicago: University of Chicago Press, 2001), 14–16.

6. Brian Cummings, introduction to BCP, xxiii.

7. Eamon Duffy, *The Stripping of the Altars: Traditional Religion in England, 1400–1580*, 2nd ed. (New Haven, CT: Yale University Press, 2005), 112.

8. Thomas Cranmer, *Defence of the True and Catholike Doctrine of the Sacrament of the Body and Bloud of*

Christ (London: Chas. J. Thynne, 1907 [1550]), 224f. Accessed via Google Books. Marion J. Hatchett notes that a late medieval devotional manual said that the role of the people in the Eucharist was simply to "see God made and eaten." See *A Commentary on the American Prayer Book* (San Francisco: HarperSanFrancisco, 1995), 353.

9. See, e.g., Duffy, *The Stripping of the Altars*, 491: "There can have been few if any communities [in the Edwardian years] in which Protestants formed anything like an actual numerical majority." A. G. Dickens had argued that throughout the sixteenth century "the growing intellectual ambitions of laymen and the extension of literacy" allowed people to see the deep attractiveness of Reformation spirituality, and these new discoveries "imposed on the English [church] hierarchy challenges which it failed to meet." *The English Reformation* (New York: Schocken Books, 1964), 12.

10. It is perhaps worth emphasizing here that these declarations were indeed meant to govern public services only, in the parish churches and cathedrals of the "realm": the preface to the 1549 *Book of Common Prayer*, which I have been quoting, concludes with a note to this effect: "It is not meant, but when men say Matins and Evensong privately, they may say the same in any language that they themselves do understand. Neither that any man shall be bound to the saying of them, but such as from time to time, in Cathedral and Collegiate Churches, Parish Churches, and Chapels to the same annexed, shall serve the congregation" (BCP 6).

11. BCP 4.

12. Attendance at Sunday services was mandated by law. The Elizabethan Act of Uniformity (1559) not only reestablished the recently proscribed *Book of Common Prayer* as the one book by which services were to be conducted, and specified punishments for priests who failed to conform to it, but also laid down fines for those who did not attend Sunday services: "All and every person and persons inhabiting within this realm, or any other the queen's majesty's dominions, shall diligently and faithfully, having no lawful or reasonable excuse to be absent, endeavour themselves to resort to their parish church or chapel accustomed, or upon reasonable let thereof, to some usual place where common prayer and such service of God shall be used in such time of let, upon every Sunday and other days ordained and used to be kept as holy days, and then and there to abide orderly and soberly during the time of the common prayer, preachings, or other service of God there to be used and ministered; upon pain of punishment by the censures of the Church, and also upon pain that every person so offending shall forfeit for every such offence twelve pence, to be levied by the churchwardens of the parish where such offence shall be done, to the use of the poor of the same parish, of the goods, lands, and tenements of such offender, by way of distress."

13. BCP 14.

14. A. Roger Ekirch, *At Day's Close: Night in Times Past* (New York: W. W. Norton, 2005), 19.

15. BCP 14, 16.

16. See, e.g., Chris Galley, "A Never-Ending Succession of Epidemics? Mortality in Early-Modern York," *Social History of Medicine* 7, no. 1 (1994): 29–57.

17. Or, if not damnation per se, eternal sentencing to the *Limbus infantium*, infants' Limbo, which was envisioned as a place not of suffering so much as emptiness—almost as frightening in its way.

    As Keith Thomas points out in his magisterial *Religion and the Decline of Magic* (1971; Oxford: Oxford University Press, 1995), some of the superstitions surrounding baptism arose from the fact that a child receives his or her name in the baptismal rite. He points out that even "in nineteenth-century Dorset some country-folk had their children speedily baptized because 'they understood that if a child died without a name he did flit about in the woods and waste places and could get no rest'" (56).

18. BCP 46.

19. BCP 73.

20. Peter Brown, *The Cult of the Saints: Its Rise and Function in Latin Christianity* (Chicago: University of Chicago Press, 1982), 65.

21. BCP 64. These are also the first words of C. S. Lewis's 1945 novel *That Hideous Strength*, where a recently married young woman cites them bitterly; she and her husband have offered little society, help, or comfort to each other.

22. BCP 66. See also, e.g., Kenneth Stevenson, "Worship By the Book," in OG, 15. It must also be noted that the corresponding passage in the wife's vows is "to love, cherish, and obey." Cranmer may have been an uxorious man, but he was also a man of his time.

23. It is even struck in the matrimonial rite, when the priest makes this demand of the bride and groom: "I require and charge you (as you will answer at the dreadful day of judgement, when the secrets of all hearts shall be disclosed) that if either of you do know any impediment, why ye may not be lawfully joined together in matrimony, that ye confess it" (BCP 65).

24. BCP 88.

CHAPTER 2: Revision, Banishment, Restoration

1. In Gerald Bray, ed., *Documents of the English Reformation* (1994; Cambridge: James Clarke, 2004), 267.

2. Cummings, introduction to BCP, xxxvii.

3. As mentioned in an earlier note, the act makes no restrictions on private prayers and allows people to "have the said prayers, heretofore specified, of Matins and Evensong in Latin, or any such other tongue, saying the same privately, as they do understand." Moreover, the act positively encourages the scholars of Oxford and Cambridge "to use and exercise in their common and open prayer in their chapels (being no parish churches) or other places of prayer, the Matins, Evensong, Litany, and all other prayers (the Holy Communion, commonly called the Mass, excepted) prescribed" in the *Book of Common Prayer*. (The exception of the Communion rite is noteworthy.) So it happened that the first language other than English that the prayer book appeared in was Latin. That version appeared in 1551, and its translator, a Scot named Alexander Alesius, was hired for the job by none other than Thomas Cranmer. See J. Robert Wright, "Early Translations," in OG, 56.

4. Both Bucer's comment and MacCulloch's agreement with its viewpoint may be found in TC, 411. This is indeed the standard scholarly view, put forth first, perhaps, in F. M. Powicke's *The Reformation in England* (London: Oxford University Press, 1941), 89ff., and warmly endorsed soon thereafter by Gregory Dix in his influential *The Shape of the Liturgy* (1945; London: Continuum, 2005), chapter 16. Dix's argument, since widely if not universally accepted, is that Cranmer had undergone, sometime around 1546, a conversion from a traditional Catholic understanding of the sacrament of Holy Communion to a fully Zwinglian one in which the rite is memorial and nothing but memorial. I think this is almost certainly true. Dix therefore sees the 1552 book as expressive of Cranmer's deepest intentions and truest beliefs; the 1549 book had been just a way station, a pause on the path to what he really wanted. Later scholars, including Diarmaid MacCulloch, have largely accepted this view. I think it plausible but by no means certain.

The most carefully nuanced account of Cranmer's thinking, on these and other matters, is surely Ashley Null's *Thomas Cranmer's Doctrine of Repentance: Renewing the Power to Love* (Oxford: Oxford University Press, 2000), the first chapter of which relates in detail the vast disagreements among scholars of Cranmer about the archbishop's core theological convictions. It must be acknowledged that Null, like MacCulloch and Dix before him, sees the 1552 Communion rite as expressing Cranmer's deepest convictions: "The ultimate expression of Cranmer's vision of

God's gracious love inspiring grateful human love was the 1552 Holy Communion service" (26).

The term "Zwinglian" derives from Ulrich Zwingli (1484–1531), the great Swiss reformer who was the first influential thinker to claim that Communion is a purely memorial and symbolic rite. This proved to be Zwingli's chief point of dispute with Martin Luther. They met in 1529 in what became known as the Marburg Colloquy but could reach no agreement on this issue, though they concurred on fourteen others.

5. Bray, *Documents of the English Reformation*, 282.

6. On the evangelical critique of exorcism, see Stephen Greenblatt, "Shakespeare and the Exorcists," in *Shakespearean Negotiations* (Berkeley: University of California Press, 1989), 94–128.

7. Quoted by Cummings, BCP 794.

8. BCP 667.

9. As Ashley Null has pointed out, "At his trial before both papal and royal officials in September 1555, Cranmer was accused of two chief doctrinal errors. He repudiated papal authority and denied transubstantiation. So important was the latter issue that previously in April 1554 the Convocation of Canterbury had arranged a public disputation, the sole subject of which was the Mass, in order that the best doctors of Oxford and Cambridge might publicly refute Cranmer, Latimer, and Ridley on their heretical Eucharistic teaching." *Thomas Cranmer's Doctrine of Repentance*, 5.

10. See Brian Spinks, "From Elizabeth I to Charles I," in OG, 45.

11. Duffy, *The Stripping of the Altars*, 589, 593.

CHAPTER 3: Becoming Venerable

1. BCP 103.

2. Even in his translations, Cranmer commonly doubles words that are single in the originals: in another confessional prayer, where the Sarum rite Latin has merely *peccata*, sins, Cranmer writes "sins and wickednesses." A collect for Good Friday says that "Our Lord Jesus Christ was contented to be betrayed, and given up into the hands of wicked men," but the original reads simply *tradi*, betrayed. As in Hebrew poetry, such parallel doubling yields both intensification of meaning and audible rhythm.

   It might also be noted that in the judgment of some of Cranmer's most acute critics, his prose is best when he translates rather than composes. G. J. Cuming notes that Cranmer "does seem to require an external stimulus to release the flow of creative activity"; this judgment is quoted approvingly by MacCulloch in *Thomas Cranmer*, 418.

3. C. S. Lewis, *English Literature in the Sixteenth Century, Excluding Drama* (Oxford: Oxford University Press, 1953), 221. Note that Lewis's own prose here takes on some of the characteristic prayer-book rhythms and patterns.

4. BCP 5.

5. As Ramie Targoff notes in *Common Prayer: The Language of Public Devotion in Early Modern England*, "Assuming the average skilled worker's weekly wage was approximately five shillings, an unbound Prayer Book would cost slightly less than half of those earnings, or the equivalent of two decent seats at the Blackfriars theater in the 1590s" (24).

The price of prayer books could be capped in this way because the government kept strict control over their printing. Only a handful of printers, carefully chosen not only for their professional skill but also for their theological sympathies, were licensed to print prayer books, though there were opportunities for them to lease their licenses to other printers. Thus a lively and highly contested market in prayer-book printing arose, complete with back-room deals, backstabbing, complaints to Parliament, and the like. This went on for two hundred years or so. The surprisingly dramatic tale is told briefly in the appendix to this book, and fully by David M. Griffiths in *The Bibliography of the Book of Common Prayer, 1549–1999* (London: British Library, 2002).

6. The term "Puritan" originally meant—as I mean it here—a person concerned to purify the worship and doctrine of the Church of England. As time went on, this category split into two: those who remained Anglicans and sought to cleanse the church from within, and those whose conscience would not allow them to remain Anglican (or who were booted out by the church). This latter group became known as Dissenters. They are to be distinguished from Roman Catholics who refused to attend Church of England services, as law required them to do: these were called Recusants.

7. *Laws of Ecclesiastical Polity* V.xxvi.2. Of the many and varied editions of Hooker's works, probably the best remains *The Works of That Learned and Judicious Divine Mr. Richard Hooker with an Account of His Life and Death by Isaac Walton. Arranged by*

the Rev. John Keble MA, in 3 volumes; 7th edition revised by the Very Rev. R. W. Church and the Rev. F. Paget (Oxford: Clarendon Press, 1888). The whole of this great monument of Victorian scholarship may be found as part of the Online Library of Liberty, here: http://oll.libertyfund.org/index.php?option=com_staticxt&staticfile=show.php%3Ftitle=921&Itemid=27.

8. In the *Complete Prose Works of John Milton*, ed. Merritt Y. Hughes, vol. 3, *1648–1649* (New Haven, CT: Yale University Press, 1962), 504.

9. Thomas, *Religion and the Decline of Magic*, 501.

10. I employ the term "high church" because of its familiarity and wide use, though in the last twenty years historians have become increasingly uncomfortable with it. Peter Lake has suggested a different name for Laud's position: "avant-garde conformity." It was avant-garde in the sense of going before general public opinion in its attempts to articulate a distinctively English, and certainly non-Roman, form of Catholicism, and in its accompanying rejection of Protestantism, but it insisted to an unprecedented degree on the need for universal conformity by the English people to the dictates of the English church. This term has become increasingly common. See Lake's essay "Lancelot Andrewes, John Buckeridge, and Avant-Garde Conformity at the Court of James I," in *The Mental World of the Jacobean Court*, ed. L. L. Peck (Cambridge: Cambridge University Press, 1991), 113–33.

11. A good brief summary of these events, and the ones described in subsequent pages, may be found in MacCulloch's *The Reformation*, 513–28. The is-

sues in church governance are masterfully explored in Anthony Milton, *Catholic and Reformed: The Roman and Protestant Churches in English Protestant Thought, 1600–1640* (Cambridge: Cambridge University Press, 1995).

12. See Henry Gee and William John Hardy, eds., *Documents Illustrative of English Church History* (New York: Macmillan, 1896), 537–45, as presented here: http://history.hanover.edu/texts/ENGref/er97.html.

13. See Judith Maltby, *Prayer Book and People in Elizabethan and Early Stuart England* (Cambridge: Cambridge University Press, 1998), 181. Maltby's book is the single best social history of the early prayer books, and I am greatly indebted to it throughout these chapters.

14. Soon after Charles's execution a book appeared, titled *Eikon Basilike, The Portraiture of His Sacred Majesty in His Solitude and Sufferings*, which purported to be Charles's reflections on ecclesiastical, theological, and political matters during his long period of imprisonment. Among other matters, it treats, and defends at length, the practice of using set forms for public worship. The book was probably written by John Gauden, who became a bishop after the Restoration, but it was widely believed to be from Charles's own hand and became a best seller. Milton's *Eikonoklastes*, quoted earlier in this chapter, was written to refute it.

15. Horton Davies, *Worship and Theology in England*, vol. 2, *From Andrewes to Baxter and Fox* (1975; Grand Rapids, MI: Eerdmans, 1996), 331.

16. Davies devotes a section of *Worship and Theology in England*, vol. 2, to the varieties of clandestine prayer-

book worship during the Interregnum and tells the stories of Sanderson and Evelyn in detail: see 352–62.

17. See Gillian Darley's fine biography, *John Evelyn: Living for Ingenuity* (New Haven, CT: Yale University Press, 2007), 102.

18. E. S. de Beer, ed., *The Diary of John Evelyn* (London: Oxford University Press, 1959), 97, 105.

19. Ibid., 406.

20. See Davies, *Worship and Theology in England*, 2:371. Davies's whole account of the Savoy Conference and its aftermath (365–73) is admirably succinct and clear.

21. See G. J. Cuming, ed., *The Durham Book: Being the First Draft of the Revision of the Book of Common Prayer in 1661* (London: Oxford University Press, 1961).

22. BCP 209.

CHAPTER 4: The Book in the Social World

1. See Roy Porter's *Penguin Social History of Britain: English Society in the Eighteenth Century*, rev. ed. (London: Penguin, 1991), especially chapter 4, "Keeping Life Going." For a more positive view, see John Walsh and Stephen Taylor's introduction to the volume they edited with Colin Haydon, *The Church of England c. 1689–c. 1833: From Toleration to Tractarianism* (Cambridge: Cambridge University Press, 1993).

2. In the second half of the eighteenth century some of the needs left unmet by the established church were addressed by the various Dissenting churches, but they were doing little more than recouping ground they had lost in the period between the Restoration

and the mid-eighteenth century, when their numbers were shrinking even in a time of significant population growth. Some of the ablest Dissenters of that period, notably Philip Doddridge and Isaac Watts, saw this worrying trend and wrote books laying out plans for spiritual renewal among the Dissenting churches. For the larger story see Michael Watts, *The Dissenters*, vol. 1, *From the Reformation to the French Revolution* (Oxford: Clarendon Press, 1978).

3. The same practice is followed in Ann Radcliffe's well-known Gothic novel *The Mysteries of Udolpho* (1794), in an early scene following the death of the protagonist's mother. "Emily checked her tears, and followed her father to the parlour, where, the servants being assembled, St. Aubert read, in a low and solemn voice, the evening service, and added a prayer for the soul of the departed. During this, his voice often faltered, his tears fell upon the book, and at length he paused. But the sublime emotions of pure devotion gradually elevated his views above this world, and finally brought comfort to his heart." Radcliffe's readers must have been gratified to note such faithful Anglican practices exhibited by a French family living in Gascony.

4. Anthony Fletcher, *Growing Up in England: The Experience of Childhood, 1600–1914* (New Haven, CT: Yale University Press, 2008), 129.

5. George Orwell, "Such, Such Were the Joys," in *Essays*, ed. John Carey (New York: Everyman's Library, 2002), 1307.

6. C. S. Lewis, "The Decline of Religion," in *God in the Dock: Essays on Theology and Ethics*, ed. Walter Hooper (Grand Rapids, MI: Eerdmans, 1970), 218.

7. Cyril Connolly, *Enemies of Promise* (1938; Chicago: University of Chicago Press, 2008), 250, 224. Even the admirably devout Edmund Bertram in Austen's *Mansfield Park*, a priest in training himself, admits the pains of college chapel services: "The greater length of the service, however, I admit to be sometimes too hard a stretch upon the mind. One wishes it were not so; but I have not yet left Oxford long enough to forget what chapel prayers are."

8. George Santayana, *Soliloquies in England and Later Soliloquies* (New York: Charles Scribner's Sons, 1922), 84. Accessed via Google Books.

9. Roger Scruton, *England: An Elegy* (London: Chatto and Windus, 2000), 92, 95.

10. In Herbert Davis, ed., with Louis Landa, *A Proposal for Correcting the English Tongue, Polite Conversation, Etc.* (Oxford: Blackwell, 1964), 15.

11. Samuel Johnson, *Prayers and Meditations*, 4th ed., ed. George Strahan (London: T. Cadell and W. Davies, 1807), 45. Accessed via Google Books. The following quotations may be found on pages 80, 81, and 155.

12. Quoted by Boyd Stanley Schlenther, "Whitefield, George (1714–1770)," *Oxford Dictionary of National Biography*, Oxford University Press, 2004; online edition, May 2010, http://www.oxforddnb.com/view/article/29281, accessed May 25, 2012.

13. From his preface to the 1784 *Sunday Service of the Methodists in North America* (Nashville: Quarterly Review/United Methodist Publishing House, 1984).

14. Quoted in Roy Hattersley, *The Life of John Wesley: A Brand from the Burning* (New York: Doubleday,

2003), 355. Hattersley's biography has been my chief source regarding Wesley's life and thought.

CHAPTER 5: Objects, Bodies, and Controversies

1. These tales were first published in the book generally known as *Hakluyt's Voyages*, more properly *The Principal Navigations, Voiages, Traffiques and Discoueries of the English Nation*, by Richard Hakluyt (published in multiple volumes between 1589 and 1600). Drake's best modern biographer, Harry Kelsey, doubts that the captain ever made it farther north than Baja California. See *Sir Francis Drake: The Queen's Pirate* (New Haven, CT: Yale University Press, 2000), especially pages 174–92.

In 1894, lovers of the *Book of Common Prayer* commissioned a 64-foot-high stone monument celebrating that first American reading of Morning Prayer and had it placed high on a hill in San Francisco's Golden Gate Park. Although it is now hard to see because of the trees that have grown up around and above it, the very existence of the Prayer Book Cross in a public park has become questioned by critics of church-state entanglements.

2. Lauren Winner documents this culture extensively in her excellent book *A Cheerful and Comfortable Faith: Anglican Religious Practice in the Elite Households of Eighteenth-Century Virginia* (New Haven, CT: Yale University Press, 2010), chapter 3.

3. Charles Hefling, "Scotland: Episcopalians and Nonjurors," in OG, 169.

4. This is Resolution 11 from the 1888 Lambeth Conference, found here: http://www.lambethconference .org/resolutions/1888/1888-11.cfm.

5. See, e.g., *Laws of Ecclesiastical Polity* V.viii.: "The Church hath authority to establish that for an order at one time, which at another time it may abolish, and in both do well. But that which in doctrine the Church doth now deliver rightly as a truth, no man will say that it may hereafter recall, and as rightly avouch the contrary. Laws touching matter of order are changeable, by the power of the Church; articles concerning doctrine not so." Hooker's theology of church order is, to an often-surprising degree, pragmatic.

6. See, e.g., Ann Blair's *Too Much to Know: Managing Scholarly Information before the Modern Age* (New Haven, CT: Yale University Press, 2011).

7. In his *Apologia* Newman described his pre-Roman position: "The Church of the twelfth century was the Church of the nineteenth. Dr. Howley [William Howley, Archbishop of Canterbury from 1828 to 1848] sat in the seat of St. Thomas the Martyr; Oxford was a medieval University. *Saving our engagements to Prayer Book and Articles*, we might breathe and live and act and speak, in the atmosphere and climate of Henry III's day, or the Confessor's, or of Alfred's. And we ought to be indulgent of all that Rome taught now, as of what Rome taught then, saving our protest. We might boldly welcome, even what we did not ourselves think right to adopt" (emphasis mine). So for Newman, the prayer book and its accompanying articles were the markers of differentiation between Canterbury and Rome. Therefore, once he became Roman Catholic he had to leave the prayer book behind.

It is not clear, to me at least, whether his affection for it was such that this abandonment cost him much pain. Certainly some recent converts from Anglicanism have felt the loss of the prayer book, and the Roman church has made room for these "Anglican rite Catholics" by authorizing an "Anglican use" that draws in part on the *Book of Common Prayer*. These provisions are most fully documented in Pope Benedict's 2010 Apostolic Constitution *Anglicanorum Coetibus*. See http://www.vatican.va/holyfather/benedictxvi/apostconstitutions/documents/hfben-xviapc20091104anglicanorum-coetibusen.html.

8. A reliable and accurate presentation of the fourth edition (1840) of the *Tracts for the Times* may be found in the Internet Modern History Sourcebook of Fordham University: http://www.fordham.edu/halsall/mod/tract03.asp.

9. See David N. Griffiths, *The Bibliography of the Book of Common Prayer, 1549–1999* (London: British Library, 2002), 23.

10. From his late essay "A Psychological Parallel," in Matthew Arnold, *Essays Religious and Mixed*, ed. R. H. Super (Ann Arbor: University of Michigan Press, 1972), 136. Arnold was so enamored of the prayer book that he once suggested that Nonconformists ought to have a prayer book of their own: "so perfectly compatible is it with all progress towards perfection, that culture would make us shy even to propose to Nonconformists the acceptance of the Anglican prayer-book and the episcopal order; and would be forward to wish them a prayer-book of their own approving, and the church discipline to which

they are attached and accustomed." From the preface to *Culture and Anarchy*, ed. Jane Garrett (1881; New York: Oxford University Press, 2009), 24. It is rather bold of Arnold to announce so confidently what "culture" wishes, but if we take his status as spokesman seriously, then culture did indeed get its wish in this respect: in 1929 the *Free Church Book of Common Prayer* appeared, taking most of its content from the 1662 book.

11. See Ian Ker, *John Henry Newman: A Biography* (1988; Oxford: Oxford University Press, 2009), 416.

12. The text of the letter may be found at the Project Canterbury website: http://anglicanhistory.org/maurice/reasons1841.html.

13. From The Right Rev. John William Colenso, ed., *The Communion Service from the Book of Common Prayer, With Select Readings from the Writings of the Rev. F. D. Maurice, M.A* (London: Macmillan, 1874). Accessed via Google Books. Colenso himself was the Bishop of Natal in South Africa and known for his radical views about polygamy, which he largely tolerated, and about the historicity of Old Testament narratives, which he largely denied. He was the defendant in one of the most famous heresy trials of the nineteenth century. His adoration of Maurice merely made it easier for people to place Maurice in the broad-church camp and thereby to dismiss him.

14. William T. Cavanaugh, "'A Fire Strong Enough to Consume the House': The Wars of Religion and the Rise of the State," *Modern Theology* 11, no. 4 (1995): 397–420. Some of the ideas of this article are developed more fully in Cavanaugh's book *The Myth*

of *Religious Violence: Secular Ideology and the Roots of Modern Conflict* (New York: Oxford University Press, 2009).

15. John Betjeman, introduction to the *Collins Guide to English Parish Churches*, rev. ed. (London: Collins, 1959), 28.

16. In writing about Neale I rely on an unpublished doctoral dissertation by Scott D. de Hart, "Anglo-Catholics and the Vestment Controversy in the 19th Century with Special Reference to the Question of Authority" (Wycliffe Hall, Oxford University, in a collaborative research program with Coventry University, 1997). Quotations here and in subsequent paragraphs are either taken from or were discovered through de Hart's thesis.

17. The "rule of contrary" is a game in which you do the opposite of what you are told to do. It is antirubrical.

   It is not my purpose here to evaluate the accuracy of the scholarship in the *Hierugia*, only to note its influence. The definitive modern work in these matters remains G. J. Cuming, *A History of Anglican Liturgy* (London: Macmillan, 1969), though it should be read in conjunction with the more recent scholarship of Nigel Yates, *Buildings, Faith, and Worship: The Liturgical Arrangement of Anglican Churches, 1600–1900,* rev. ed. (1991; Oxford: Clarendon Press, 2000), and with Eamon Duffy's *The Stripping of the Altars*, much cited earlier in this book.

18. Quoted in Roy Jenkins, *Gladstone: A Biography* (New York: Random House, 1997), 384.

19. One of the ways Neale and like-minded folk indicated their traditionalism was by antique spelling: "rubrick"

rather than "rubric," "fabrick" rather than "fabric,"
and, above all, "Gothick" rather than "Gothic."

CHAPTER 6: The Pressures of the Modern

1. "Editor's Note" to *The Prayer Book Interleaved with Historical Illustrations and Explanatory Notes Arranged Parallel to the Text*, by W. M. Campion and W. J. Beamont (London: Longmans, Green, 1898). Accessed via Google Books.

2. Hatchett, *A Commentary on the American Prayer Book*, 10.

3. BCP 32.

4. C. S. Lewis fought against changes on such grounds right to the end of his life, when changes to the prayer book were coming to seem inevitable. In a 1961 article he wrote, "The old Prayer Book prayed that the magistrates might 'truly and indifferently administer justice.' Then the revisers thought they would make this easier by altering *indifferently* to *impartially*. A country clergyman of my acquaintance asked his sexton what he thought *indifferently* meant, and got the correct answer, 'It means making no difference between one chap and another.' 'And what,' continued the parson, 'do you think *impartially* means?' 'Ah,' said the sexton after a pause, 'I wouldn't know *that*.'" But of course Lewis, as he surely understood, was stacking the deck by using a rural example, since people in rural communities are always more linguistically conservative than those in cities, and by invoking the opinion of a sexton, a person who certainly would have had lifelong acquaintance with the prayer book's liturgies. The essay is "Before We Can Communicate,"

in *God in the Dock: Essays on Theology and Ethics* (Grand Rapids, MI: Eerdmans, 1970), 254.

5. Quoted in Alec Vidler, *The Church in an Age of Revolution* (1961; London: Penguin, 1990), 163.

6. The fullest and best exploration of this psychic shock remains Paul Fussell's *The Great War and Modern Memory* (New York: Oxford University Press, 1975).

7. Vera Brittain, *Testament of Youth* (1933; Harmondsworth: Penguin, 1989), 360.

8. Ibid., 453.

9. Robert Graves, *Good-Bye to All That*, rev. ed. (Garden City, NY: Doubleday, 1957), 199ff.

10. Thus when, after the next war, in his famous essay "Politics and the English Language," George Orwell wants to denounce the use of stale political clichés, he writes, "A speaker who uses that kind of phraseology has gone some distance toward turning himself into a machine. The appropriate noises are coming out of his larynx, but his brain is not involved as it would be if he were choosing his words for himself. If the speech he is making is one that he is accustomed to make over and over again, he may be almost unconscious of what he is saying, as one is when one utters the responses in church." *Essays*, 963.

11. Vidler, *The Church in an Age of Revolution*, 158.

12. Horton Davies, *Worship and Theology in England*, vol. 5, *The Ecumenical Century* (1970; Grand Rapids, MI: Eerdmans, 1996), 294.

13. Bryan Spinks, "The Prayer Book 'Crisis' in England," in OG, 240.

14. The well-known irony here is that "thee" and "thou" are the familiar forms of the second-person pronoun,

meant to indicate intimacy rather than formality. While two forms of second-person address remain common in other European languages, the distinction underwent a long slow decline in English, though it was still maintained in rural and some northern English communities well into the twentieth century. The novels of D. H. Lawrence often testify to this.

The sudden appearance of the phrase "thees and thous" in the mid-Victorian era is evident through a search of Google's Ngrams Viewer: http://books .google.com/ngrams/graph?content=thees+and +thous&year_start=1800&year_end=2000&corpus =0&smoothing=3.

15. The prayer is one of the most famous in the prayer book, and in its most familiar form reads as follows: "We do not presume to come to this thy Table, O merciful Lord, trusting in our own righteousness, but in thy manifold and great mercies. We are not worthy so much as to gather up the crumbs under thy Table. But thou art the same Lord, whose property is always to have mercy: Grant us therefore, gracious Lord, so to eat the flesh of thy dear Son Jesus Christ, and to drink his blood, that our sinful bodies may be made clean by his body, and our souls washed through his most precious blood, and that we may evermore dwell in him, and he in us. Amen" (BCP 33). It first appeared in the 1549 book, having been written by Cranmer, working from various liturgical and biblical sources. It appears in almost all prayer books until the 1960s, but at various locations in the Communion rite.

16. Quoted in Vidler, *The Church in an Age of Revolution*, 166.

17. Betjeman, introduction to the *Collins Guide to English Parish Churches*, 79.

18. *Laws of Ecclesiastical Polity* V.57.5. Hooker differs from the Roman and the Lutheran views of the sacrament not by denying the Real Presence but by denying that we can specify *how* Christ is present: "The fruit of the Eucharist is the participation of the body and blood of Christ. There is no sentence of Holy Scripture which saith that we cannot by this sacrament be made partakers of his body and blood except they be first contained in the sacrament, or the sacrament converted into them. 'This is my body,' and 'this is my blood,' being words of promise, saith we all agree that by the sacrament Christ doth really and truly in us perform his promise, why do we vainly trouble ourselves with so fierce contentions whether by consubstantiation, or else by transubstantiation the sacrament itself be first possessed with Christ, or no? A thing which no way can either further or hinder us howsoever it stand, because our participation of Christ in this sacrament dependeth on the co-operation of his omnipotent power which maketh it his body and blood to us, whether with change or without alteration of the element such as they imagine we need not greatly to care nor inquire" (V.67.6). Dix does not quote Hooker on these matters but probably should have.

19. Dix, *The Shape of the Liturgy*, 670.

20. Ibid., 613. Here I will explore the influence of Dix's work on modern prayer books, without passing judgment on its scholarly adequacy. That would be a topic for a different book.

21. Dix, *The Shape of the Liturgy*, xxxii. Dix habitually declines to capitalize words such as "christian" and "christianity."

22. Dix, *The Shape of the Liturgy*, 672.

23. Colin Buchanan, "The Winds of Change," in OG, 231.

24. When this union was being negotiated in the preceding decade, one of the most vocal Anglican opponents of it, and of its being recognized as valid by the Church of England, was none other than Gregory Dix.

25. Lesslie Newbigin, *The Gospel in a Pluralist Society* (Grand Rapids, MI: Eerdmans, 1989), 147. The "Christian primer" to which I refer is *Sin and Salvation*, originally published in Madras in 1956. Newbigin wrote much of the book in Tamil and then, because of time pressures, switched to English and had a friend translate the remainder into Tamil.

    One of the greatest griefs of Newbigin's long and brilliant career was the persistent failure of the Anglican Communion to offer full acknowledgment of, and to declare full communion with, the Church of South India. This is especially ironic in view of the later influence of the CSI on Anglican worship worldwide. See Geoffrey Wainwright, *Lesslie Newbigin: A Theological Life* (New York: Oxford University Press, 2000), 9.

26. For a detailed account of this work, see T. S. Garrett, *The Liturgy of the Church of South India: An Introduction to and Commentary on "The Lord's Supper,"* 2nd ed. (1952; Oxford: Oxford University Press, 1954).

27. The texts of those resolutions may be found at the Lambeth Conference website: http://www.lambeth

conference.org/resolutions/1958/. Here is Resolution 73: "The Conference welcomes the contemporary movement towards unanimity in doctrinal and liturgical matters by those of differing traditions in the Anglican Communion as a result of new knowledge gained from biblical and liturgical studies, and is happy to know of parallel progress in this sphere by some Roman Catholic and Reformed theologians. It commends the Report of the Sub-committee on the Book of Common Prayer on this subject to the careful study of all sections of the Anglican Communion." And Resolution 74:

> The Conference, recognising the work of Prayer Book revision being done in different parts of the Anglican Communion,
> (a) calls attention to those features in the Books of Common Prayer which are essential to the safeguarding of our unity: i.e. the use of the canonical Scriptures and the Creeds, Holy Baptism, Confirmation, Holy Communion, and the Ordinal;
> (b) notes that there are other features in these books which are effective in maintaining the traditional doctrinal emphasis and ecclesiastical culture of Anglicanism and therefore should be preserved;
> (c) and urges that a chief aim of Prayer Book revision should be to further that recovery of the worship of the primitive Church which was the aim of the compilers of the first Prayer Books of the Church of England.

Point (c) suggests that the lessons of Dix's *Shape of the Liturgy* had not been universally acknowledged. And both resolutions show less resolve than anxiety.

CHAPTER 7: Many Books for Many Countries

1. This letter was posted online by the current leadership of St. Mark's Church in-the-Bowery as part of their campaign to get funding from the Partners in Preservation project. I reposted an image of it here: http://ayjay.tumblr.com/post/23287582837/auden-expresses-himself-on-then-experimental. Auden's literary executor, Edward Mendelson, confirmed the authenticity of the letter for me and provided an approximate date.

2. He then added, "But in beauty, in poetry, he, and St. Jerome, the great Latin translator, are beyond all whom I know." C. S. Lewis, *Reflections on the Psalms* (New York: Harcourt, 1958), 7.

3. Walter Hooper, ed., *The Collected Letters of C. S. Lewis*, vol. 3, *Narnia, Cambridge, and Joy, 1950–1963* (San Francisco: HarperOne, 2007), 1222.

4. Ibid., 1594.

5. The websites from which these statements are taken are, respectively, http://prayerbook.ca/, http://pb-susa.org/, and http://www.pbs.org.uk/.

6. BCP 32–33.

7. The equivalent prayer in the English *Alternative Service Book* reads: "Almighty God, our heavenly Father, we have sinned against you and against our fellow men, in thought and word and deed, through negligence, through weakness, through our own deliberate fault. We are truly sorry, and repent of all our sins.

For the sake of your Son Jesus Christ, who died for us, forgive us all that is past; and grant that we may serve you in newness of life to the glory of your name. Amen."

8. Hatchett, *A Commentary on the American Prayer Book*, 344.

9. See http://www.churchofengland.org/prayer -worship/worship/texts/introduction.aspx.

10. I must confess that I could not think more highly of this volume, which I use every day. It is essentially an Anglican version of a Catholic breviary, such as monks might use to say the Daily Office. Anglican adaptations of the breviary have been made for some time now, but before *Common Worship: Daily Prayer* were invariably highly Anglo-Catholic in character. The liturgical altitude of the Common Worship is adjustable.

11. Stewart Brand, *How Buildings Learn: What Happens after They're Built* (New York: Viking Penguin, 1994).

APPENDIX: The Prayer Book and Its Printers

1. What follows is a summary taken largely from David N. Griffiths's remarkable *The Bibliography of the Book of Common Prayer, 1549–1999* (London: British Library, 2002).